DYNAMIC DUOS
Of the Bible

Glenn Sprich

Copyright © 2020
Glenn Sprich
Saint Louis, Missouri

All Rights Reserved

Library of Congress Control Number: 2020904906

ISBN 978-1-7341682-5-9

No part of this publication may by reproduce in any form or by any means without prior written permission from the author except that brief portions may be quoted for a review.

Correspondence and orders may be sent to:

Glenn Sprich
www.biblestudiesforthecommonman.com
studiesbibleglenn@gmail.com

DEDICATION

This book is dedicated to the "duos", the partnerships of men and women in this book who struggled together with their daily lives, their accomplishments, with their faith and with their relationship with God. Some to serve God, some to serve themselves.

DYNAMIC DUOS of The Bible

CONTENTS

	Acknowledgments	i
	FORWARD	1
1	ADAM and EVE	3
2	CAIN and ABEL	9
3	JOSEPH and HIS BROTHERS	17
4	SAMSON and DELILAH	25
5	RUTH and NAOMI	33
6	DAVID and GOLIATH	43
7	DAVID and JONATHAN	51
8	AMNON and TAMAR	61
9	AHAB and JEZEBEL	71
10	MARY and JOSEPH	79
11	SIMEON and ANNA	89
12	JAMES and JOHN	95
13	MARY and MARTHA	109
14	ANANIAS and SAPPHIRA	119
15	AQUILA and PRISCILLA	127
16	PAUL and TIMOTHY	137
	FINAL THOUGHTS	143
	SOURCES	145

ACKNOWLEDGMENTS

This is the second publication in the "Bible studies for the common man" series. Special thanks go to some of the same people who contributed and made possible the first book in the series, "The Greatest Five" and some additional people specifically made a contribution to this second study. Thank you to both groups, for your continued support and expertise along your friendship. Without your help this Bible study would not have been possible.

Special thanks to:

My wife Patti, my life partner who said "You're writing another book!" yet encouraged me to take the time and the effort to write a second time.

My writing coach Janet Kraus who was adamant that after you write one book, write another book. Also, she created the web site "Bible studies for the common man" to help promote this book.

My editor Edie Greishaber who for over twenty years served as secretary and office manager of the Lutheran Church of Webster Gardens. She currently serves as the editor and writer of our daily congregational devotion series. Edie is an example of being both a Martha, serving God's church with her abilities and as Mary serving with love and caring for the people of God.

My friend Jane Zyk from Webster Gardens Lutheran church who provided additional editing giving the book its final review.

My daughter in law Laura Sprich who designed the front and back covers of this book. You can't express enough the importance of the front cover which attracts readers to look at your book and the back cover which gives a glimpse into the books unique content.

My friend Dottye Buethe who serves in our church library on Sunday mornings. She has tirelessly promoted the sale of my first book and is "The Greatest Five"s best salesman!

Finally, thanks to Steve Menke of No Waste Publishing, an imprint of Accent Group Solutions.

FORWARD

There is a verse in Ecclesiastes chapter four "Two are better than one…" In the following verses it goes on to explain that two can accomplish far more together as a pair than by themselves as individuals. As you look at each "Dynamic Duo" in this study you will discover that the two of them together complimented each other, helped each other, lived life together, had a specific impact on their faith together, and uniquely effected God's people and His church. Also in this study you will read that some of the "Dynamic Duos" complimented each other but in a harmful and destructive way. They too were "better than one" but in an evil, sinful way, hurting God's people and His church. We learn from both examples, the famous and the infamous.

Whether the "Dynamic Duo" was famous or infamous, these pairs together left their mark on the history and development of God's people and His church. Their life lessons, their faith lessons, their accomplishments still effect us today.

It is inconceivable to think about each individual person in this book without the other. Where would Adam be without Eve? We sure would not be here! Mary as a single mom without Joseph? Timothy without Paul to guide him in the true doctrines of our faith? David without Goliath? That event propelled David into the course of becoming the greatest king of Israel.

The "Dynamic Duos" in this study are about two separate people, living separate lives, drawn together by God to achieve His purpose. Each person had their own unique strengths and unique weaknesses of personality and faith coming together at a specific time in the history of the Bible. God put them into partnerships of life and faith. God also puts us into partnerships of life and faith with our spouses, our friendships, our co-workers, our neighbors and sometimes even strangers! In every relationship, partnership you encounter in life, may God Bless your lives, your faith, your service to His people and His church.

CHAPTER 1

ADAM and EVE

"The Consequences of Sin"

And the Lord God commanded the man, "You are free to eat from any tree in the garden; but you must not eat from the Tree of Knowledge of Good and Evil, for when you eat from it you will surely die."
GENESIS 2:16-17

Adam and Eve were God's greatest achievement in all of creation. He saved the best for last and created them in His own image. They were His image of love, intelligence, emotion, skills and choice. God gave man a free will, and He gave man the responsibility of obeying Him and living under His direction. By staying true to His will, Adam and Eve had the perfect life in paradise as God intended. But Adam and Eve had other ideas of what free will meant. By choosing the opposite of God's will and direction, they chose a life outside of their perfect garden in a world filled with pain, suffering and death.

Their Story…

Genesis 1:26-31 In the final act of Creation God made them man and woman, created in His image to rule over the earth. Man had all of creation at his disposal. He was to reign over the plants, the trees, the fish, the birds, the animals. All that God provided in the garden would be the perfect environment for Adam and Eve to help them grow and multiply. God looked at His creation and saw that it was good.

Genesis 2:8-9   God created the earth and put Adam and Eve into a beautiful garden that would sustain them and that they could enjoy. In addition to all the trees and plants in the garden, God created a special tree of life, a tree containing the knowledge of what was good and what was evil.

*For thought...*What does having free will mean to you? What responsibilities come to us along with the gift of free will?

Genesis 2:15-17   God directed Adam and Eve to work and take care of His garden and use anything in it. He gave them one exception: they were not to eat the fruit from the tree of knowledge of good and evil because if they did, they would die.

Genesis 3   One morning as Eve was walking in the garden, the Serpent approached her and said, "Did God really say that you couldn't eat from every tree in the garden?" Eve replied, "God told us not to eat from the tree of knowledge of good and evil. If we do eat that fruit, we will surely die." The Serpent was crafty and wanted to encourage Eve to question God's authority in her life. "You won't die. If you eat from the tree of knowledge, you will be as wise as God is. You will know the difference between good and evil and you, too, will be just like God." Eve walked up to the tree of life, and saw how beautiful the fruit was and picked one of the pieces of fruit from the tree and took a bite. It was delicious! She turned to Adam, "Adam, this fruit is the sweetest-tasting, most beautiful fruit in the garden. Here, take a bite." Adam reminded Eve of what God had said: "Eve, we are forbidden to eat this fruit." With insistence, Eve spoke the words told to her by the Serpent. "We won't die if we eat this fruit. We will become like our Creator, as gods ourselves. We will be able to decide what is good and what is evil." She holds the fruit out in front of him: "Here, let's become gods together." Adam took the fruit and bit into it. Instantly, they both realized what they had done! They were not gods. Instead they felt shame for what they had done. Hurt and guilt swept over them. They could not even look at each other, let alone face God in their nakedness, so they covered themselves with leaves to try to hide their shame.

For thought...The Serpent, the father of all lies, put Adam and Eve to the test of their free will. Why did they choose to disobey God and chose, instead, to obey a lie? Did Adam and Eve really know that they were making a choice between life and death and what the consequences would be? God specifically told Adam and Eve that choosing to eat from the tree of life would result in their deaths. Satan told them that by eating the fruit from the tree of life would mean that they would never die. By following a lie, Adam and Eve chose death. After eating the forbidden fruit, Adam and Eve were not like God; they were not even in God's perfect image any more. Even before God confronted them about what they had done, Adam and Eve hid. They knew they had chosen the path of disobedience to God and sin instead of the perfect path that God had laid out before them. What tactics does Satan use in your life which makes you vulnerable to sin and temptation?

The next day as God was walking through the garden, He couldn't find Adam or Eve. They were usually eager to greet Him every morning but on this morning they were nowhere to be found. So God called out, "Adam! Eve! Where are you? Why aren't you saying "Good Morning" to Me like you usually do?" Adam, who must have been filled with dread at the thought of facing God that day, responded: "I heard You, Lord, but I couldn't face You. I did something wrong, and I was afraid to see You." "Adam, why are you hiding from Me? What did you do that has caused you to feel such fear and shame? You've never had that feeling before, have you? But we both know that there is only one reason you could be feeling afraid to face Me. Did you eat from the tree of knowledge of good and evil?" Adam, who had made a covering for himself and Eve out of leaves, slowly came out of the bushes where he was hiding. He told God that Eve had eaten the fruit from the tree and told him it was the sweetest fruit she ever had. "And God," he continued, "she said it would make us more like You ... like a god." At that, Eve slowly emerged from her hiding place in the bushes wearing a covering of leaves. As God turned toward her, she could barely lift her eyes to face Him. She struggled to speak the words: "The Serpent told me I would be a god if I ate it, so I ate it. It wasn't true. The Serpent lied to me. It's his fault."

One thing was sure about what the Serpent had said ... now Adam and Eve really did know what was good and what was evil. They had known only good before, but now their eyes had been opened to also know evil because of their disobedience.

For thought... Can you imagine what it will be like to be physically present with God, walking and talking with Him as you stroll together in the Garden?

God drove Adam and Eve out of the garden paradise into a harsh pain filled world as a consequence of the sin they committed. The lives of all mankind changed forever.

God had the perfect plan for His world—a plan for eternal life a perfect relationship with Him. Man challenged that perfect plan by choosing a way that was contrary to God's plan of eternal life in paradise. By their choice, Adam and Eve chose Satan's plan which led, instead, to suffering and death.

For Thought... Even before Adam and Eve were driven from the Garden of Eden, God already had a plan to restore all mankind to eternal life and a perfect relationship with Him. What was God's plan?

THE DISCUSSION

1.) What did Adam and Eve hope to gain that they didn't already have by eating from the tree of knowledge of good and evil? How would their lives have been different if they had not partaken? What did they think God's reaction would be?

2.) Man was made in the image of God. He has given each of us intellect, emotion, skills, choice and the ability to love. Adam and Eve were also given responsibility to work and obey God. We, too, are made in the image of God. What does that mean to you? What are our responsibilities being made in the image of God?

3.) Adam and Eve chose to disobey God; they gave in to sin and temptation. There were grave consequences for their choice. There are serious consequences for our choices to give in to sin and temptation in our lives today. Think about a time when you gave in to temptation and sin. What were the immediate and what were the long term consequences for your choice?

4.) What are some of the steps we can take to fight temptation and sin in our lives? What are the positive consequences of resisting temptation and sin?

5.) God has already paid the price for our sin through the life and death of His Son. How does the knowledge of, and faith in God's plan of salvation through Jesus Christ, help us deal with our sin on a daily basis?

THE ACTION

1.) Do you deal with persistent sin in any area of your life? Ask God for forgiveness; develop a plan to to stop that cycle of sin; ask a friend to hold you accountable.

2.) Begin each day with Scripture and with prayer to arm yourself against the power of Satan and sin.

3.) Each day give God thanks that you have been made in His image. Show love, mercy and forgiveness to others. Serve God and your neighbor. Make choices that honor and obey God.

THE PRAYER...

Dear Heavenly Father,
Thank You for creating us in Your image, to love and to serve You and all people we meet. Help us fight sin and temptation in our lives and help us daily to make choices that please You. And most of all, thank You for sending Your Son Jesus as our Savior. Thank You that through Him You restored our relationship with You as our Heavenly Father. Amen

CHAPTER 2

CAIN and ABEL

"Living in a World of Violence"

Now Cain said to his brother Abel, 'Let's go out to the field." While they were out in the field, Cain attacked his brother Abel and killed him."
GENESIS 4:8

We live in a violent world. Wars, fights, shootings, killings and more are a part of our everyday lives. Every time we listen to the news or read a paper, we hear about war escalating in another part of the world or another drive-by shooting in our city. Or worse ... we hear of a mass killing in a school or place of worship. There are many reasons people resort to violence. Some people use violence for revenge; others are driven by mental illness. Still others just want to hurt people to feel better because they are hurting themselves. No matter what the reason, all acts of violence are acts of sin.

God sees every act of sin as grave, especially acts of violence. Recorded in the Book of Genesis in the Bible, is one of the worse acts of violence possible. It is the taking of another person's life. We're not certain what caused Cain to commit the extreme act of murder. It certainly could have been jealousy, hatred, revenge, or even mental illness. But we do know that when Cain committed murder, he was acting under Satan's control, not that of His Creator. Once Adam and Eve left the Garden of Eden, they left behind the love, peace and protection of paradise God had provided for them. They, in effect, entered into a world where Satan reigned and where there was violence, suffering and death.

Their story...

Genesis 4 As part of their commission from God at Creation, Adam and Eve were to be "fruitful and multiply." In other words, they were to have children and populate the earth with their family. As a consequence of their sin against God they committed in the Garden, Eve was told that childbirth would be hard and painful for her. When she was writhing and crying out in the excruciating pain of giving birth to Cain, her firstborn child, Eve must have wondered what childbirth would have been like before sin entered the world. Adam was told by God that he would have to "break his back" working the soil to create food for himself and his family. He, too, when digging in the dirt with calloused hands and sweat dripping from his forehead, must have had moments when he remembered how perfect life in the Garden was before he sinned against God.

Cain was the first child of Adam and Eve. Later they had another child, another son Abel. We don't know how many other children that Adam and Eve had but there were probably significant numbers of other children born to them. Additional children of Adam and Eve are mentioned in this chapter and also in Chapter 5 of Genesis. There are continuing generations of their family so that within a span of perhaps 100 plus years there could have been over 100,000 people on the earth. Remember, Adam lived for 930 years and had a son, Seth, when Adam was 130!

Agriculture was the primary source of food and other products to sustain life. Cain chose to be a farmer, tilling, planting and working the soil to produce grains, vegetables and fruits. Abel chose to raise animals, sheep, goats, cattle. While they were in the Garden, God told Adam and Eve to subdue, to have control over the earth (soil) and all its abundance and over all animals on the land and fish in the sea. Outside of the Garden, that commission from God changed and required that Adam and Eve and each member of their future family would work long hours, drenched with sweat and pain to now subdue the earth.

While living with the consequences of their sin, Adam and Eve still had a relationship with God. They were no longer "walking with Him in the Garden in the cool of the day", they were working hard to produce crops and animals to sacrifice to Him and to worship, honor and please Him. Adam and Eve knew that all things come from God. Without His blessing the ground to produce food as a result of their labor or His blessing the animals so they reproduced offspring to grow their flocks, Adam and Eve and their family would have nothing. Adam and Eve taught their children to respect God. They taught their children to obediently sacrifice their best grains and produce. Also, their best and most perfect animals to honor God and give Him thanks for sustaining their lives. Every week Cain went into his fields and picked out grain and vegetables to offer as a sacrifice to God, Likewise, Abel chose a suitable sacrifice from his flocks. Abel was sure to choose the largest, fattest, most perfect animal to give to God. Together, as their parents had taught them, Cain and Abel laid their gifts on a stone altar as a sacrifice and as a thank offering to God for all He had provided for them.

But something was not right. Abel's offering, Abel's sacrifice, was consumed by fire as a symbol of acceptance by God. But Cain could not get his sacrifice on the altar to burn! Cain was mad. He thought to himself, "Isn't my sacrifice good enough? Don't I come here every week with my sacrifice for God? Why does He not burn my offering? Why is it that the animals offered by Abel are always accepted by God but God won't accept my gifts?" Every time Cain looked over at his brother's sacrifice burning with its thick, fragrant smoke curling into the air and lifting up to God in heaven, Cain "burned" with jealousy and hate towards his brother. He thought that God had made Abel His favorite.

For thought…How do you feel when you give your best to God, serving His church, helping His people?

God saw that Cain was upset about his sacrifice. "Cain, why do you burn with anger? Why do you go around depressed all day? Could it be that you're not doing the right thing? Could it be that you're not giving Me your best grains and produce but that you are keeping them for yourself instead? You're just giving Me the leftovers, stuff you would throw in the trash. Don't you think that if you gave Me your best offering that I would burn it, too? Be careful with your anger and attitude. It could get you into trouble someday."

For thought…Do you ever feel jealous of the accomplishments of people in your family, friends or people at work and at church? How can you deal with that? How should you feel?

One morning, Cain said "Abel, why don't you come with me and help me pick out the best grain and the best fruit for my sacrifice. I want my offering to be as pleasing to God as yours is and completely burnt up to worship Him." As they were walking to the fields, Cain was so consumed with hatred for his brother that he picked up an enormous rock and struck Abel in the back of his head, killing him instantly. There was blood everywhere. Quickly, Cain dug a shallow pit and put Abel's body in it and covered it with rocks.

When Cain was finished burying his brother Abel, he heard God's voice: "Cain, where's your brother Abel? I saw the two of you leave together this morning." "I don't know where he is. I don't keep track of what he does all day," Cain snapped back. "Cain, are you sure about that? What do you mean you don't know where Abel is!" God shouted back. "I heard Abel's cry as you crushed his skull with a rock! His blood is everywhere! Now listen to Me. Because you killed your brother You are now a cursed man. The ground not only contains your brother's blood but because of that, there will be no more crops; nothing from you will grow from the earth ever. You will live by what you can scrape off the ground or pluck from trees. Get out of here … now!" "Lord, please have mercy on me. I won't be able to survive life like this, I'll die. If I don't starve to death, other people will kill me because of what I did to Abel." "I won't let anyone kill you, Cain. See, I put a mark on you. When other people see you, they will recognize that mark and they won't hurt you. If they do, they'll be sorry." Cain packed up his belongings and wandered off into the hills.

THE DISCUSSION

1.) Why does it seem like there is so much more violence in the world today? Why do some people choose to kill to settle disputes or because they are angry about life? We know there are other ways to handle problems or disputes. Think of a time when you "burned with anger" about something or someone. How did you handle your anger?

2.) If you are a victim of violence or abuse, how do you cope with that? Where can you go for help?

3.) For what reason(s) might Cain have believed he had to kill Abel? How could Cain have resolved his anger and jealousy without killing Abel?

4.) Abel was a good man (mentioned in Hebrews 11); yet, his brother killed him. Why do bad things, violence and abuse happen to good people?

5.) There is physical abuse happening to people all around us. How do we recognize that this abuse is happening? What can we do to help stop it?

THE ACTION

1.) Support organizations in your community that help victims of violence.

2.) If you have abused or hurt someone, ask God and that person to forgive you.

3.) Pray about it and try to resolve the harm or abuse you received from someone. Seek counseling if needed.

THE PRAYER

Dear Heavenly Father,
Violence is everywhere in our world today. Please stop the hurt and pain that causes people to act out with violent behavior. Help us to reach out to others with love, forgiveness and mercy when they hurt us or others. Let those who are hurting and have thoughts of revenge or suffer with mental illness, turn toward You for help. Keep them from harming others and themselves. And, dear Heavenly Father, please protect us and our families from evil and violence in this world. In Jesus' name, Amen.

CHAPTER 3

JOSEPH and HIS BROTHERS

"A Lesson in Forgiveness"

But Joseph said to them, "Don't be afraid. Am I in the place of God? You intended to harm me, but God intended it for good to accomplish what is now being done, the saving of many lives. So then, don't be afraid. I will provide for you and your children." And he reassured them and spoke kindly to them.
GENESIS 50:19-21

One of the most important teachings of Jesus, second only to loving the Lord God with all your heart and loving your neighbor as yourself, is the teaching of forgiveness. Forgiveness is a hard concept for us to understand and put into practice. Our human nature is to seek revenge against someone who has hurt us, someone who has caused us pain. We want to lash back at those who hurt us. The story of Joseph and his eleven brothers in the Old Testament is the classic example of how to forgive those who have hurt us.

Their story...

Genesis 37-50   Joseph lived in Canaan along with his eleven brothers. They were the sons of Jacob and his wives. Jacob did what no parent should ever do; that is, favor one child over the others. He even flaunted it by giving Joseph a special coat! Because he was made to feel so set apart by his father, Joseph thought of himself as a pretty special kid, born of his father's favorite wife. He was good looking, smart and a little cocky. He even predicted that one day his brothers would bow down and worship him!

Then came a day when his brothers had enough of his arrogant talk and actions. They grabbed Joseph and were going to kill him. But the oldest brother, Reuben, just couldn't agree with such a drastic act against his own brother, so they sold Joseph into slavery. They were convinced that they would never see him again. They told their father Jacob that Joseph had been killed by a wild animal. Jacob was so overcome with grief that he vowed to grieve the rest of his life until he died.

For thought... If you were one of Joseph's brothers, how would you have reacted to your father's preferential treatment and love for Joseph? How would you have reacted to Joseph's arrogance?

That was not the end of Joseph's story ... actually, just the beginning! Joseph ended up in Egypt working for a high official in the Egyptian government. True to his form, handsome, young, and bright, Joseph worked his way up to be the house manager of an Egyptian official. He is falsely accused of fooling around with his master's wife and thrown into prison. While in prison, guess what, he does it again! He does such a good job as an administrator in the jail that he is placed in charge of the jail! During his time in prison he met two fellow prisoners--a cup bearer and a baker who both worked in the household of Pharaoh but had fallen out of favor. They both had unusual dreams while they were in prison which they could not understand. They knew Joseph was a bright guy so they approached him to see if he could interpret their dreams. Joseph did foretell one prisoner was to be restored to his original position in Pharaoh's house and the other prisoner was to be hanged. Years later Pharaoh had a similar disturbing dream and none of his advisors could help determine what it meant. The cup bearer, who was restored to his former position as Joseph had predicted, told Pharaoh about this guy in prison who could interpret dreams. So Pharaoh sent for Joseph. Again, true to form, Joseph told Pharaoh what the dream meant. He told him that the whole world would have a famine in seven years including Egypt. So, Pharaoh put Joseph in charge of storing enough food over the next seven years to counter the effects of the expected famine. His advanced knowledge and preparation for the famine saved both Egypt and the whole world from starvation.

For thought…Have you ever faced a difficult situation in your life that God turned into something good for you? How did that affect you and your faith in God?

During the years of famine, Jacob sent ten of his sons to Egypt, the only country in the world that had food they could buy. While his brothers were in Egypt looking to buy grain, Joseph recognized them! Joseph, of course, did not look like his brothers any more. He had acquired the dress and appearance of a high official in Egypt, so his brothers would never had recognized him. When he was face-to-face with his brothers, Joseph accused them of being foreign spies. They pleaded with him, explaining that they were from Canaan. They further explained that they were a family of twelve brothers: ten there, one brother back home (Benjamin) and one brother who had died (Joseph). Joseph then ordered one brother to be held as a hostage in prison until this younger brother, still at home, could vouch for them and verify their story. The brothers were in despair. How could this have happened to them? How could they explain it to their father? There was only one answer: God was punishing them because they had the blood of Joseph on their hands. They were convinced they were finally receiving the justice from God they deserved for killing Joseph.

The nine brothers returned home and brought their youngest brother back to Egypt with them to verify their story.

When Joseph saw his brother Benjamin for the first time in over ten years, he was overcome with emotion. The brothers collected the grain and started to head back home. But, Joseph had other ideas. He had in mind a plot to secretly accuse Benjamin of stealing as a ploy to bring him back to Egypt. A silver cup was found in Benjamin's possession and he was accused of stealing from Pharaoh. Benjamin and his brothers were arrested, returned to Egypt and brought before Joseph. Joseph could not contain himself any longer. He broke down crying right in front of them. Because they did not recognize him as their brother, they could not understand what was happening. This high government official who accused them of stealing is crying uncontrollably.

For thought...Instead of forgiving his brothers, what should Joseph have done according to human law and custom? What would we have done if we were in Joseph's position?

Joseph excitedly throws off his officials hat and robe of office and yelled, "It's me, Joseph, your brother! It's really me! I can't believe we're all together again after all these years! Look at you, my brothers, here in Egypt. I can't believe it! I have to know... Is dad still alive?"

His brothers were scared to death. Their heads were spinning; they couldn't comprehend what was happening. Again, Joseph tells them, "It's me, your brother Joseph! Remember back to that horrible day when you sold me as a slave? God was with me, and He protected me. He brought me to Egypt and even made me second in command to Pharaoh in charge of the storing and distribution of food. It was because of God's intervention that Egypt and all other countries were spared the devastating effects of the famine which we are now experiencing. Get all your families and animals together. We'll find a place right here in Egypt for you to live at least until the famine has ended. You and your families will be taken care of.

No worries!" When the brothers returned home and told their father that Joseph was alive, Jacob was overcome with joy. He came to Egypt together with his entire family. And after so many years, he once again was able to embrace his lost son, Joseph.

For thought...In Romans 12:17-21, Paul gives us some pretty tough guidelines to follow about forgiveness. What are they? How can we actually live up to those standards?

THE DISCUSSION

1.) Why is it so hard for us to forgive someone who has hurt us? What do we give up by forgiving that person? What do we gain by forgiving that person?

2.) What do you feel in your heart when you forgive someone? What do you feel in your heart when you do not forgive someone who has hurt you?

3.) Do you need to forgive and forget? Can you forgive the person who hurt you, without forgetting the hurt?

4.) How do you respond to the words of Jesus who said if you do not forgive the sins of those who hurt you, God will not forgive your sins?

5.) How do you deal with someone who has hurt you and doesn't want your forgiveness?

THE ACTION

1.) Is there anyone you have hurt that you need to ask for forgiveness. Ask God to give you the courage to go to that person and seek his/her forgiveness.

2.) If someone that has hurt you has died, you need to forgive them. Consider making restitution with them by writing your thoughts down as if you were talking with that person. Pray and ask God to work forgiveness in your heart.

3.) Be an example of Christian forgiveness to others.

THE PRAYER

Dear Heavenly Father,
Help us to follow the example of Jesus and Joseph on how to forgive those who have hurt us. Help us to get rid of the burden of hurt and pain and revenge. Sow Your peace into our hearts; provide healing for our pain. Forgive us when we have hurt You or someone else by our words or actions. Teach us to show love and kindness to everyone we meet. In Jesus name. Amen

CHAPTER 4

SAMSON and DELILAH

"A Destructive Relationship"

With such nagging she prodded him day after day until he was sick to death of it. So, he told her everything. "No razor has ever been used on my head," he said, "because I have been a Nazirite dedicated to God from my mother's womb. If my hair was shaved, my strength would leave me, and I would become as weak as any other man."
JUDGES 16: 16-17

Visions of lust and love come to our minds just by speaking their names, Samson and Delilah! Samson, the strongest man in the world and judge of Israel; Delilah, the beautiful and manipulative Philistine seductress. From the very beginning of their relationship until the very end of their lives, they preyed on the weaknesses of each other. Samson's weakness was for beautiful women, and Delilah's weakness was for money. Instead of complementing each other as a loving couple should, they chose instead to destroy their relationship and each other out of their own selfishness and desires.

Their story...

Judges 13-15   Samson was a judge of Israel for twenty years. Whenever Israel sinned by worshipping foreign gods, God would punish them usually by sending another nation to oppress them. Israel would then cry out to God for help, and God would then send a deliverer, a judge, to rid Israel of its oppressor. This cycle of sin and deliverance went on for hundreds of years. Samson was one of God's appointed judges … chosen to deliver the Israelites from the oppression of the Philistines.

An angel of God one day appeared to Samson's mother (she was barren, unable to have children) and told her she would give birth to a son. From then on she knew that one day her son Samson would do something special to serve God and His people. The angel told Samson's mother that he would be a Nazirite vowed to serve God. As part of his vow to God, he would follow special rituals, not drink alcohol, eat certain foods and he was never to cut his hair. From the time of his birth, the Spirit of God stirred in him. Through the years Samson grew into the strongest man ever born. While he had great courage, he also had a will that was stubborn and followed his own lusts and desires. He began his adult life by marrying a Philistine woman against the wishes of his parents. While Samson was away, she was given to another man in marriage by her father. Samson then began to make frequent visits to see the local prostitutes. Ultimately his weakness for women and sex would lead to his downfall and death.

In spite of his weaknesses, Samson accomplished some great things for Israel. He became a one-man army harassing one of Israel's greatest enemies, the Philistine people. His numerous encounters with the Philistines resulted in death for many of the enemy. On one occasion, Samson killed 1,000 Philistine men with the jaw bone of a donkey.

Judges 16 One day while visiting the city of Gaza, Samson went to his favorite place in town, the local brothel. As he entered the house, he immediately turned his eyes toward the corner of the room where he spied a beautiful young woman, he "wanted." Samson quickly ushered across the room to her, sweeping aside her perspective client. He took his place as her new client and spent a portion of the night with this unnamed "working girl." Meanwhile the Philistines had discovered his whereabouts and were waiting to capture him when he came out of the brothel at dawn. But Samson, learning of their plan, escaped by breaking down the city gates foiling the plan to kill him.

In what may have been a scenario much like the one described above, he visited another brothel in the Valley of Sorek where he saw a beautiful young woman named Delilah. He was smitten with her and, in fact, fell in love with her. This "working girl," however, had ambitions of her own!

For thought…What special or unique gift has God given you? How are you using it in a way that serves God and helps others?

The Philistines were always scheming and attempting to get their revenge against Samson. They tried several times to subdue him but they failed each time. They were so frustrated that they tried a new approach, money. They went to Delilah, Samson's love partner and made a proposition she couldn't refuse. They promised to make her a wealthy woman if Delilah would reveal to them why Samson was so strong. Delilah took their offer.

For thought…Do you have any habit or personality trait that is annoying or even harmful to your spouse or to your marriage? What steps can you take to go about changing or eliminating it?

Three times Delilah prodded Samson. "Tell me the secret of your great strength and how you can be tied up and subdued." Three times Samson taunted her with foolish answers about how to subdue him. Three times each attempt failed with Delilah crying out in frustration: "You lied to me;

you embarrassed me in front of all my friends. Tell me now. Why are you so strong?" Delilah is feeling desperate and crushed. She can feel the money slowly slipping through her fingers so she mounted one more campaign to get Samson to confide in her. She pulled out her trump card, "Samson, if you really love me like you say you do, prove it to me by telling me the truth about your strength. If you don't tell me right now, I'm leaving you!" Samson couldn't take it anymore. All the nagging and threats had worn him out. His ability to resist was gone! He looked Delilah in the eye and told her, "Alright, alright! I'll tell you. I am a Nazirite which in Israel means, I was born with a special gift and a special responsibility. My strength is given to me by God. In return, I have vowed to serve Him and to refrain from ever cutting my hair as a sign of obedience to Him. Cut my hair and poof, my strength is gone. Now please stop nagging me. Leave me alone." Delilah knew by the sound and sincerity of Samson's voice that this was finally the secret to his strength.

Delilah immediately sent word to the Philistine leaders and told them to come to her house one more time. She finally had the answer about how they could get Samson. In her message to them, she was sure to add, "And by the way, bring the money you promised me." The next day as Samson was sleeping, Delilah had Samson's hair cut off. After his haircut, Delilah shook him to wake him and screamed, "Samson, get up! Get out of here. The Philistines have found out where you were living and are here to kill you!" Samson jumped up and immediately knew something was different. He reached back behind his head and…no hair! It was gone. "Oh God, what has happened to me?" Just then five guys jumped him, tied him up and just for spite, gouged out Samson's eyes. They got him, they finally got him. The mighty Samson—blind, weak and at their mercy. They had gotten their revenge. They took their prize back to Gaza and put Samson in prison.

For thought…How do we get rid of the shame and guilt when we commit a sin that we know was a bad choice? What are the consequences of that sin along with the guilt and shame?

Every day people of Gaza would parade by Samson's cell in prison, making fun of him. They spit at him, threw garbage at him and shouted insults and profanities, "Where's your strength now Samson? Where's your people's God now! Your God and your people have abandoned you! Our god is greater than your God. The Philistine people are the masters over Israel and you can't do anything about it!"

At the Philistine's annual festival to honor their god Dagon, they brought Samson to the city temple where the party was going on to have Samson "entertain" them. People were laughing, and throwing wine and food at Samson, their prize catch. Samson asked the Philistine servant who was holding his chains if he would put Samson between the two front pillars that were supporting the temple so he could lean on them for support while standing up. What the Philistines didn't observe but that Samson could feel, was that while he was in prison, his hair had started to grow back! As Samson put his hands on the stone columns, he said a quiet prayer to God, "Dear Lord, please forgive me for breaking my vow. Please give me Your Spirit and Your strength one last time to punish those who oppress Your people." Using all his strength, Samson pushed the two columns apart and caused the entire two-story temple to collapse killing more than 3,000 Philistines. Samson was also killed by the collapsing stones of the temple to Dagon. It was a tragic end to a violent and misguided life. Was Delilah present that day at the temple celebrating with her fellow Philistines the demise of Samson? Did she witness the spectacle of Samson? What might she have been feeling as she saw Samson, her blinded and humiliated lover, push aside those temple pillars?

THE DISCUSSION

1.) Samson and Delilah did not have a loving relationship. What are some of the traits and characteristics of a loving Christ-centered marriage?

2.) Samson had strength and power and a weakness for sex. Delilah had the strength of beauty and a weakness for money. How do you help build up the strengths of your spouse? How do you deal with and understand the weaknesses of your spouse?

3.) There was no trust between Samson and Delilah. They were in a relationship together only to satisfy their own needs. They could not trust the actions or motives of each other. Why is trust between spouses so important in a marriage? Why is meeting the needs of your spouse so important in marriage?

4.) What effect does pornography, infidelity, chat rooms and social media have on our marriages today? How do you recognize that these are causing a problem in your marriage?

5.) What actions can you take to honor, serve and value your spouse each day to make them feel special and loved?

THE ACTION

1.) List three things that you can start practicing that would make you a more caring and loving husband or wife.

2.) Take time to schedule date nights together, just to talk and have fun together.

3.) Talk to other Christian couples about the challenges they face in marriage. Ask how their faith has bonded them together as a couple.

THE PRAYER

Dear Heavenly Father,
Thank you for the blessing of our spouses. Help us to honor, to respect, and to love our wives or husbands every day. Thank You that we share our Christian faith and that our shared faith makes our marriage stronger. Help us to prevent any barriers from coming between us as a couple and for our marriage to be an example to other couples. Amen.

CHAPTER 5

RUTH and NAOMI

"The Importance of Family"

> But Ruth replied, "Don't urge me to leave you or to turn back from you. Where you go, I will go, and where you stay, I will stay. Your people will be my people and your God, my God."
> RUTH 1: 16

One of the greatest love stories in the Bible is not about the love between a young man and a young woman. It is about the love between a mother-in-law and her daughter-in-law! We often make fun of in-law relationships in families, but the relationship between Naomi and Ruth is one of sacrificial and unconditional love. Because of their love and respect for each other, they were able to put the welfare and happiness of the other person ahead of their own. They entrusted their lives to one another. In doing so, they have shown us the importance of loving, God-fearing relationships in the family.

Their story...

Ruth Chapter 1 Naomi and her husband Elimelek, along with their two sons, lived in the town of Bethlehem in Judea. Because of a famine in their homeland of Israel, they moved to the nearby country of Moab. While they were living in Moab, Naomi's two sons married women from that country, Orpah and Ruth. Sometime later Naomi's husband and both her sons died, leaving the three women widowed. Faced with a dismal future in a foreign land, Naomi decided to return to her home in Bethlehem. Naomi encouraged her daughters-in-law to stay in their home country where it would be easier for them to marry again. But because of their great love and devotion to her both Orpah and Ruth desired to stay with Naomi no matter where she went. While Naomi was grateful, she was certain there was no future for either of them in Israel. So she insisted that they both stay in Moab. Naomi knew that without a husband or sons, there would be no one to provide for her or her daughters-in-law. She knew they would be forced to beg for food and shelter and to rely on the generosity of others to survive. And she also knew there was a strong possibility that they would die if no one came to their aid. Orpah then decided to stay in her home country of Moab, but Ruth insisted that she still wanted to go with Naomi regardless of what the future might bring. Ruth's pledge to Naomi is a beautiful expression of her deep love and loyalty: "Where you go, I will go. Your people will be my people. Your God will be my God. Where you will be buried, I will be buried." Wow, what devotion! So, Naomi and Ruth said goodbye to Orpah and journeyed to Bethlehem. Upon their return to Bethlehem they were greeted by the entire town. "After all these years, Naomi, you're back. It's great to see you! Naomi, where is Elimelek? Where are your sons?" Naomi replied, "They're all gone, they're all dead!! I have come back with nothing, nothing. The only person I have left in my life is my daughter-in-law Ruth. I went away trying to start a new life in Moab but God didn't bless me. In fact, He took everything away from me-my husband, my sons and my home. I don't feel like Naomi any more. That person is gone. She doesn't exist anymore. From now on call me Mara, Bitter. That's how my life has turned out."

For thought... Why do you think Orpah and Ruth developed such love for their mother-in-law? And why do you think Naomi loved Orpah and Ruth like her own daughters?

Ruth Chapter 2 Once they arrived back in Bethlehem, Ruth began to make plans for their lives there. She said to Naomi, "We need to eat. Let me go into a field and pick up the leftover grain after the daily harvesting." It was a custom to let poor people or foreigners passing through the area pick up the small broken pieces of grain left or dropped by the field workers. Their gleanings could at least provide some food for them to eat. (Leviticus 19: 9-10) Ruth was concerned about Naomi because of her age and health so she had her stay behind: "Naomi, you stay here; it's really hard work, bending over all day under the intense sun. It's too much for you. I'll be okay. I'll find food somewhere for us." Naomi agreed and sent Ruth on her way to gather grain but told her to be careful. Naomi was concerned that the owners of the fields may not like having a young woman from Moab gleaning in their fields. Ruth left Naomi and went to a nearby barley field to gather grain that day. Naomi knew it would take all day for Ruth to gather enough scraps to put together a meal for one person, much less for two people. She knew Ruth would need to work twice as fast and twice as long to gather enough grain to feed both of them for the day.

She also knew that Ruth was going into a very hostile environment. Not only was she a stranger, but she was also a Moabitess. (Israel and Moab became enemies when the Moabites refused to help the Israelites when they returned from Egypt.) As Ruth picked up scraps of barley, Boaz the owner of the field where she was gleaning, caught a glimpse of her. Boaz knew his workers and had never seen this girl before. He asked some of the workers who was that young woman and he learned it was Ruth, Naomi's daughter-in-law from Moab. The workers told him Ruth had been working hard all day long, taking only a short break, not even stopping to eat or drink anything.

Later that morning, Boaz approached Ruth: "Young lady, you can continue working in my field where you will be safe. I will make sure that no one will bother you and when you get thirsty, feel free to get a drink of water from my jars." Ruth bowed as a sign of respect and humility and replied,

"Dear sir, I'm a foreigner, even lower than a servant. Why are you being kind to me? I really don't deserve it." Boaz responded, "Ruth, isn't it? Gossip travels fast and I've heard all about you and Naomi. You gave up everything to come back to Bethlehem with Naomi, your mother-in-law, who isn't even your blood relative. May God bless you for your love and devotion to her." "Thank you, sir, for your kind words!" said Ruth.

At lunch time Boaz came over to Ruth and invited her to take a break: "Come over and have a sandwich with us." Ruth accepted his invitation and took a break. She ate a portion of the sandwich given to her, saving the remainder to take home for Naomi. As Ruth headed back to the field, Boaz instructed all the workers, "Don't hassle her or even go near her. I also want you to pull out some extra stalks of grain and leave them on the ground in front of her. Make it easy for her to find them and pick them up." As a result, Ruth came home with a large sack of grain after only one day's gleaning. It was more than she could normally have gleaned in a week! (She was unaware of the instructions Boaz had given to his field workers to leave excess grain for her.)

When Ruth got home, Naomi could hardly believe it. "Look at all that grain! And you brought me leftovers, too. How thoughtful. How did you gather so much today?" Ruth explained, "I was working in the barley field across the valley and the owner of the field was very kind to me. His name is Boaz." Naomi replied with excitement in her voice. "Oh my gosh, Boaz! He is a member of our clan, a relative. He may even be a kinsman-redeemer who can help us." Ruth continued telling Naomi that Boaz had told her to stay in his field working each day during the harvest with the other women as a worker, not as a poor gleaner. He promised that she would be safe and that no one would bother her. So every day Ruth went into the field with the other women workers and collected grain during the harvest.

*For thought…*When Naomi heard about Boaz, what might have been going through her mind?

Ruth Chapter 3 Toward the end of the harvest, Naomi shared some thoughts with Ruth, "I think I may have found a home and a future for you. Boaz is a relative of ours and a special one at that. And as a bonus, he isn't married. He'll be hard at work all day and night at the threshing floor winnowing the barley after the harvest tomorrow. Get washed, put your best clothes on, do your make-up and fix your hair so that you look super attractive. Now listen to me. You may not understand this, but do exactly as I say. It's a strange custom, but if you follow my instructions, Boaz will know what to do to help us."

After a successful hard day's work and dinner, Boaz laid down, exhausted, on the threshing floor and fell asleep. As Naomi had instructed her, Ruth lay down next to Boaz on the threshing floor and took part of the blanket covering him to also cover herself. Expecting to be alone, Boaz was startled, woke up and found Ruth, lying next to him. He didn't recognize her at first because she was all dolled up with a fancy hairdo and makeup. He asked, "Who are you? What are you doing lying next to me?" "I'm Ruth," she said, "the woman to whom you showed kindness as I worked in your field. I am here to ask you to 'cover me' with your care, to be my family's kinsman-redeemer." (Deuteronomy 25:5-10)

Boaz responded: "I know what you're doing; it's a custom with which I am familiar. Did Naomi tell you what to do?

Anyway, you've made an honorable request. You are a wonderful woman, Ruth, with a great reputation. You could have your pick of a lot of guys for a husband; yet, you picked me. Don't be afraid, trust me. There is a family kinsman-redeemer closer in line than I am. Stay here tonight. Leave right before daybreak. I'll go see him right away in the morning. If he accepts his responsibility as a kinsman-redeemer, then you must marry him. If he doesn't accept it, then I will exercise my right as next in line. I will honor my obligation as your kinsman-redeemer. (Boaz had a plan. He knew this other relative's situation. If Boaz was correct, he would end up as the kinsman-redeemer for Ruth.)

Ruth followed Boaz' instructions and spent the night on the threshing floor. She left at daybreak, unseen, with a bag full of goodies from Boaz. When Ruth arrived at home, Naomi wanted to know how everything went. Ruth reported that everything had gone according to Naomi's direction, including Naomi's knowing what Boaz would do. "Now let's wait and see what happens tomorrow," responded Naomi encouragingly. "Boaz is a man on a mission. He knows what he is required to do. We can count on him, he'll do the right thing."

For thought... Why did Naomi think her plan would succeed?

Ruth Chapter 4 Early the next day Boaz went to the city gate where business and legal transactions took place. There he met his relative, the first in line family kinsman-redeemer. Boaz greeted him and bowed respectfully: "Please sit down. A business and family matter has come to my attention. You may not be aware of this. One of our kinsmen, Naomi, wife of Elimelek … you remember Elimelek don't you? … she recently came back to Bethlehem from Moab where she has lived for quite a few years. She's a widow now, so she needs to sell the piece of land her husband owned. Because our conversation is a business transaction, I've asked the town elders to witness our meeting. You are number one in line to redeem and purchase this family land from Naomi. If want to buy it, go ahead. If you don't want to buy it, (redeem it) then as next in line after you, I will buy it." The guy said, "Sure, I'll buy it, no problem." "By the way," added Boaz, "did you know that Naomi has a daughter-in-law, Ruth the Moabite widow? She is of marrying age. Along with the purchase of the property, you are obligated to marry her as kinsman-redeemer. She is a member of Naomi's family so you must provide an heir to the property you are buying to keep it in Elimelek and Naomi's family." The guy replied, "What! I can't do that. It would mess up my whole family's inheritance and future just to help Naomi and that Moabite girl. I support a wife and kids now. I can't support another set of a wife and kids and get nothing for it! No thanks! She's all yours!"

As part of an old, yet recognized custom (the rite of Halitzab) the first kinsman-redeemer took off his sandal and handed it to Boaz signifying his transfer of responsibility to Boaz. "There you go Boaz. Good luck to you. I'm out of here." Boaz took the sandal and addressed the elders: "You witnessed this transaction today. I, Boaz, will buy the property of Elimelek and his sons from Naomi, and I will marry Ruth the Moabite widow to continue their family lineage."

As a happy ending to the story, Boaz and Ruth marry and have a baby boy, Obed, who happens to be the father of Jesse, and the grandfather of King David! Naomi is blessed with a grandson and received the praise of everyone in Bethlehem who finally realized how blessed Naomi was to have Ruth as a daughter-in-law. It was even better than having seven sons! Ruth, the devoted daughter-in-law is honored by God. She became part of the lineage of Jesus, one of only four women mentioned in the genealogy recorded in Matthew's Gospel.

For thought...Naomi was praying for a husband and a future for Ruth. What might Boaz have been praying for all those years before meeting Ruth?

THE DISCUSSION

1.) Naomi and Ruth went through some really tough situations in their lives. They kept trusting in God to help them through those rough times. Why did they, and why do we, continue to trust God during the trials we face in life?

2.) When we encounter a difficult or challenging situation in life, why do we need to both pray about it and then take some action like Naomi and Ruth did?

3.) Naomi, Ruth, and Boaz had difficult decisions to make in their lives. When we are faced with difficult decisions in life, how do we know the right thing to do? What is the value of doing the right thing even though it may be hard to do?

4.) How important is it to have a Christian family? How does it affect your faith?

5.) Naomi, Ruth, and Boaz all showed sacrificial love toward each other. How do you show sacrificial love to your friends and family?

THE ACTION

1.) Think back to the tough times in your life. How did God help you through those times.

2.) List some of the promises and commitments you made to your family and to God.

3.) Be a "kinsman-redeemer" to someone in your family who could use your love and help.

THE PRAYER

Heavenly Father,
We trust You in all situations in life, both in the good times and in the bad times. Help us especially during the tough times to stay close to You and strong in our faith. Help us to recognize others in need all around us and to reach out with our love and with Your love for them. And thank You, Heavenly Father, for our families and the love and blessings that we share each day. Amen!

CHAPTER 6

DAVID and GOLIATH

"Dealing With Adversity"

"Your servant has killed both the lion and the bear; this uncircumcised Philistine will be like one of them, because he has defiled the armies of the living God."
1 SAMUEL 17: 36

During our lifetime we will probably face many difficult people and many difficult situations that have the potential to hurt us emotionally, harm us physically or even become life threatening. These people and situations challenge us to not only trust in God for His help and protection, but also to act appropriately in response to these life experiences. Look at David and Goliath ... talk about a life-threatening adversary, a life-threatening situation... How about taking on a nine-foot giant trained like a Navy Seal when you are only a teenager! But David was no ordinary teenager. He had a strong faith in God and good hunting and fighting skills learned while out alone in the fields near Bethlehem tending his sheep. He also trusted in God's strength and promises to protect him. While Saul and his soldiers only saw the physical size and strength of Goliath, David knew the "size and strength" of God. He knew that with God's strength and protection he could defeat Goliath both physically and spiritually. As we face our own "giants" in life, we need to stay focused on God and the "power" we have in Him as well as the faith and abilities that He has given us.

Their story...

1 Samuel 17   The Israelites are once again at war with their arch enemy, the Philistines. Following a custom in ancient warfare, a champion warrior from each opposing army would meet and do battle to determine the outcome of the war. Instead of a bloody and costly fight between the two armies, only these two soldiers would fight. The army whose warrior killed his opponent would be victorious. The army of the losing warrior would be forced to submit and surrender to the winning side. In the battle recorded in 1 Samuel 17 a nine-foot giant named Goliath came forward to represent and fight for the Philistine army. He challenged any of the soldiers in the army of Israel to come out and fight him.

For forty days Goliath came out each morning and shouted insults at the army of Israel, "You men of the Israeli army, you're here every day with your King Saul, looking for a fight. Here I am, a Philistine warrior, your enemy. Let's do this. Someone, anyone, come and take me on. If he kills me, our people will serve your people. If I am the victorious, Israel will serve us. You cowards, you dogs, I curse you and your no-good God! Fight me right now, today, or submit to us as our slaves!"

No one wanted to fight Goliath, he was three feet taller and probably 100 or more pounds heavier than any Israeli soldier. Israel had many brave, experienced soldiers, but going against Goliath was like going on a suicide mission. Saul even went so far as offering money and even his daughter in marriage to any of his men who would fight Goliath (and survive!).

David was in the camp of Israel's army that day bringing some food and wine to his older brothers who were in Saul's army. As David was dropping off the supplies and talking to his brothers, he witnessed Goliath shouting, cursing, and ridiculing Israel and their God. David was mad! Angry feelings welled up inside of him, "This heathen is making fun of our army, but more importantly, he's making fun of our God." His older brother Eliab grabbed David by the tunic. "Shut up, little brother. Go back to your sheep. Did you just come here to see if one of us will be killed in battle? You are too cocky for your own good." He shoves David to the ground. But David jumped up, shook the dirt off and quickly retorted, "All I did was bring you some food and wine because dad told me to. Can't I even say anything about what's going on here?" A couple of other soldiers heard the encounter between David and his brothers. They thought David might want to repeat what he told his brothers to King Saul. Saul sent for David. David bowed to the king, and said, "My King, I look around here at your army and all I see is defeatism. I will go and fight Goliath! I can beat him!" Shocked, the king replied "Look at you, you're just a little kid. Goliath is an experienced soldier. He's killed a lot of men. Get out of here and go back home." David looked directly at Saul and said with conviction "Yes, I am just a teenager. Yes, I am just a shepherd. But I tend my father's flocks in the hills of Bethlehem. More than once, I have taken on both a lion and a bear when they tried to eat one of my father's sheep. A bear and a lion are a lot more dangerous than this Philistine loudmouth. God protected me then. I know He will protect me now." Saul was convinced: "Well then, go ahead and fight Goliath, you'll need all the luck and protection God will give you. Are you sure you know what you're doing? "

For Thought…When we face our "Goliaths", our difficulties in life, why should our first move be to turn to God for guidance on what to do?

After David received Saul's blessing to fight Goliath, a couple of Israeli soldiers tried to put heavy armor, a helmet and a shield on David for use in the battle. But the heavy armor weighed as much or more than David! "I can't use these things," David replied, "They will be a hindrance and not a help. Take 'em off! Let me fight the way I know how to fight."

David left the camp and started walking down the hill into the valley between the two camps. He saw the massive size of Goliath in the distance. David thought he really is a big guy! But David had a plan of attack. He stepped over a small stream at the base of the valley and stooped down and picked up five smooth, good sized stones each a little smaller than the size of a baseball. Goliath saw this young shepherd boy coming toward him. Goliath moved forward until the two of them were separated by about ten yards. The "giant" cried out, "What are you doing here? Are you crazy? Who are you? What do you think I am, just an ordinary soldier? Look at me! Just because you're an athletic kid, do you really think you can beat me? Are you the best your army can send to fight me? I curse and spit on you; I curse and spit on your God. I'm going to squash you like a bug so there will be nothing left of you but some blood and guts!" David was not shaken but shouted back with confidence, "You come at me with your size, your strength, and your array of weapons, but I am armed with something better than all of the weapons you have. I have something more powerful, I have God on my side. His protection and His strength are my weapons. Nobody, nobody beats my God! Today, right now, right here, I'm going to avenge all the profanities you have spoken against our army and our God. You're not going to cut me down, just the opposite is gonna happen. I'm going to cut you down, and the wild animals are going to feed off of your body, not mine. Everybody here, everyone in my army and everyone in your army, will witness that Israel worships the true God, the living God. He will win today, and you and the Philistine army will lose today." Goliath is enraged. He puts on his helmet, raises his shield, and grasps his spear. He is combat ready! As he moves closer to David, David reaches into his bag and pulls out one of the stones he picked up. David runs forward and twirls his slingshot around and around as fast as he can and then at the right moment, David lets loose and off the stone shoots traveling at unbelievable speed and accuracy. Smack! A bull's eye! The stone hits Goliath in the forehead right between the eyes. Goliath is stunned. He sees stars; he staggers backward. Dizzy, he blacks out and falls backwards to the ground! Before Goliath comes to, David quickly runs over, picks up Goliath's sword and with one blow, cuts off Goliath's head! Can you see it now? David then picked up Goliath's head and held it high in the air for everyone in each army to see. The army of Israel went wild. He did it, he killed Goliath. The cheering army shouts, "Let's get those Philistine scum!" They run after the fleeing Philistine army and annihilate them.

*For thought...*David was armed only with a sling shot and five stones taking on Goliath. With what does God "arm" us with, what weapons do we have when we come face-to-face with our problems and challenges in life?

After the battle, Saul asks his general, "Whose kid is that? What family does he come from? Why did he come here?" Not sure of the answer, General Abner replied, "I've never seen him before. He's not one of my regular soldiers. But I'll find out who he is and I'll get him for you." General Abner finds David surrounded by Israeli soldiers congratulating him, patting him on the back and brings him to see King Saul. Saul says, "Young man, what an amazing fight! What family do you come from young man and who is your father?" David proudly says, "My father's name is Jesse. Our family is from Bethlehem."

*For thought...*Sometimes in our lives, our "Goliaths" defeat us; the marriage fails, the illness is terminal, our children leave the faith. How do you deal with adversity when it seems to overpower you and not turned out the way you wanted or prayed about?

THE DISCUSSION

1.) Think back to when you have faced your "giants" in life like illness, job loss, divorce or death. How has God specifically helped you through those difficult times?

2.) Why is it important to face our fears and problems in life and not run away from them?

3.) Do you have people in your life who sometimes criticize you, belittle you or even bully you? How do you deal with those people?

4.) How do you keep yourself from becoming discouraged and stay strong when you do what you think is right or when you stand up for your Christian values even though other people disagree or get angry with you?

5.) How can you help your spouse, family member, friend or coworker who might be battling a difficult problem or situation in their life?

THE ACTION

1.) Take time today to thank God for helping you though a difficult time in your life.

2.) David had a plan to defeat Goliath. Have a plan and pray about how you can prepare for the difficult battles in life.

3.) Pray daily for your family and friends as they are going through the "Goliath's" in their lives.

THE PRAYER

Dear Heavenly Father,
When we face the "Goliaths," those overwhelming problems in life, we ask that You be with us. We can't face them alone; we need Your love, Your Spirit, Your direction, and Your strength to help us through them. We also ask You to give us the love, the strength and the caring needed to reach out to others who are struggling with "giants" in their lives. In Jesus' name, Amen

DYNAMIC DUOS of The Bible

CHAPTER 7

DAVID and JONATHAN

"Importance of Friendship"

"How the mighty have fallen in battle! Jonathan lies slain on your heights. I grieve for you, Jonathan my brother; you were very dear to me. Your love for me was wonderful, more wonderful than that for a woman."
2 SAMUEL 1: 25-26

God gives us our families but our friends are the families we choose. Just as choosing a spouse can make or break your life, so can your choice of friends. Life offers many opportunities to make friends. Friendships often develop around a shared experience or a common interest. Some friendships develop quickly while others take years to develop. Whatever the circumstances, friendships are some of the most important relationships that God gives us. David and Jonathan had a God-directed relationship. Their strong friendship developed around shared life experiences demonstrated in humility, loyalty and sacrifice. Both David and Jonathan demonstrated their love for each other and their intense love for God. At the same time, each of them experienced pain and tragedy in their lives. While the experiences that David and Jonathan could have driven them apart, instead it drew them closer. In the end, they each achieved greatness. Although Jonathan was the rightful heir to the throne of Israel and might have been Israel's greatest king, it was instead David who became Israel's greatest king.

Their story...

1 Samuel 18:1-4 As we begin the story of David and Jonathan, you might recall from an earlier chapter of this study that David had just killed the giant of the Philistine army, Goliath. Scripture tells us that following that encounter with Goliath, Jonathan and David became best friends. Jonathan was a brave and experienced soldier himself. In fact, history records that he once single-handedly attacked a Philistine outpost and killed twenty men in hand to hand combat! Jonathan had been keenly aware of the daunting challenge facing David when he took on Goliath. After all, David was just a teenager and a shepherd at that! He wasn't a trained soldier. But clearly, Jonathan recognized the courage, the hunting skills, the confidence, the love of God and country, and the strong, trusting faith that David had. Jonathan also had many of those same qualities himself. Perhaps that was one of the reasons, they meshed together as friends so quickly and so closely. As a token of his care and concern for David, Jonathan gave David his own battle gear (swords, bows, uniforms). These were expensive and hard to come by especially for a poor shepherd boy. By Jonathan giving David his army equipment, Jonathan put David's safety and welfare in battle above his own. Another important part of their commitment to one another was a sworn allegiance that their friendship and families would be joined together forever.

*For thought...*David was a shepherd. Jonathan was the prince of Israel. Does it matter that our friends are of different social classes, different ages, different races? Do you have friends who are of different backgrounds?

1 Samuel 18:1-30, 1 Samuel 19:1-7 David has now transitioned from a lowly shepherd to an accomplished soldier and commander, winning tremendous victories against the enemies of Israel. The people of Israel celebrate David's victories as greater than King Saul's victories. Saul was king of Israel and he should have been his country's greatest warrior and commander. But because of the battlefield success of David, Saul became furious of this shepherd turned soldier. He burned with jealousy and could not have this young "competitor" in his palace. One day this jealousy was so intense in Saul that he tried to kill David, but God was with David and he was able to elude every assassination attempt by Saul. Saul even goes so far as giving orders for his son Jonathan to kill David. Jonathan could not believe it. He told his dad that David had never done anything wrong. He affirmed David's love for his king and country by recounting David's victories in battle time after time. Jonathan even reminded Saul that David did the impossible and killed Goliath and brought a great victory that day to Israel. There was no reason to kill David because David was loyal to King Saul and his family. Saul calmed down and assured Jonathan that David would not be killed.

*For thought…*From the perspective of parents, how important is it that our children choose good friends? How do we reinforce the good friendships our children have? How do we guide our children away from friends who may be a bad influence on them?

1 Samuel 20: 1-42   Unfortunately, Saul's oath to his son not to kill David didn't last very long! Saul was so consumed with hate and jealousy toward David that he sent some of his men to kill him. And once again, God protected David and he was able to escape. (David's escape this time was made possible with the help of Michal, Saul's daughter and David's wife!) Following that escape, David met with Jonathan. David wanted some answers. "Why is your father still trying to kill me? I have never threatened him in any way." Stunned, Jonathan quickly replied: "He isn't trying to kill you. My father tells me everything. If he were trying to kill you, I would know." David was not convinced. "Your dad knows that you and I are best friends. Out of all people, you are the one person he wouldn't tell. He wants me dead, Jonathan." Eager to protect David, Jonathan asked how he could help David. David had a plan to test whether Saul's intentions were deadly or not and suggested that he stay away from the family dinner that night at the palace. If Saul became angry about David's not coming to dinner (so Saul and his men could kill David), that would be a sign to Jonathan that Saul was planning to assassinate David. If Saul did not get angry because of David's absence, that would be a sign that he was not planning to murder David. Jonathan agreed to the plan although he was still confident that if his father were trying to kill David, he would know. In spite of his confidence, however, his primary concern was to protect David from harm. Jonathan came up with a plan and safe way to let David know if he is in danger of being killed. The plan was that the next day following dinner, Jonathan would leave the palace in the morning and practice his archery. The direction and distance that Jonathan shot his arrows, would be the sign for David of Saul's intent to harm David or not. They then embraced one another. David encourages Jonathan, "Remember, we swore an oath of friendship with each other. We love each other as brothers but if you think I deserve to die, like your father wants, then kill me right here, right now!"

"I love you as a brother I could never do that. I am being completely honest with you. I believe that my father means no harm. God has brought us together as friends. As your friend, I promise I will talk with my dad about you and I will let you know what I learn. I pray that God blesses you as He has blessed me and my family. Your friendship has been a valued source of God's blessings for me and my family these past years. As a soldier I may get killed one day, David, swear to me that you will continually love me by taking care of my family. I pledge my life in friendship for you." David responded, "Jonathan, I too, pledge my life in friendship for you and your family."

That night at dinner, Saul asked where David was. Jonathan responded as David directed him to. Jonathan told his Father that David has asked if he could miss dinner with us and go back home to Bethlehem for a special sacrifice with his family. Saul jumps up and screams in a rage, "Jonathan, you dog! I know you conspired with David against me. This son of Jesse wants my kingdom, and yours. Now get out of here now, find David and kill him." Jonathan leaps up from his table, screaming back at his father, "What has David ever done to you? Why do you want to kill him? You have no reason other than your jealous inadequacies!" Saul, became even more enraged, shouted out profanities, grabs a nearby spear and throws it at Jonathan, his own son! He barely missed and threatened Jonathan," I'll kill you, too, you traitor!" Jonathan runs out of the palace in anger and disgust, fully aware that David's suspicions about his father Saul were true.

The next day Jonathan went out to practice his archery as part of the plan to send David a signal letting him know if his life was in danger. David emerged from his hiding place in the field and the two met. They looked at each other trembling and in tears putting their arms around each other and embraced, knowing that their lives, friendship and relationship would never be the same. "David," Jonathan said, "God has brought us together; God will always bless our friendship and no matter what happens to us, our friendship will hold our families together, forever."

For thought…Are most of your friendships more short-term, lasting months or a few years depending on your circumstances or are most of your friendships more long-term, lasting over the course of many years or your lifetime? Does it matter? What's good about each?

1 Samuel 23: 16-18   This section of Scripture details a remarkable expression of love and devotion for David on the part of Jonathan. He shares with David what he believes God's plan is for the future: "Don't worry, David. My father is not going to kill you. You, David, are going to be the next king of Israel some day, not me. As Saul's oldest son, you know that I am in line for the throne. That's one reason my father wants you to die to keep our family on the throne of Israel, not your family. But I would rather be your right-hand man than king of Israel! My Dad knows exactly how I feel."

*For thought...*What a remarkable statement by Jonathan! Have you ever had a situation where you put your friend's welfare and interests before your own? Why were you able to do that?

1 Samuel 31:1-3   The Philistines were again in battle with Israel. Saul led his army out to fight but things did not go well for Saul and Israel's army. Israel was defeated, and Saul was killed along with Jonathan and his two brothers.

*For thought...*David and Jonathan's friendship ended when Jonathan was killed. What are some of the other reasons that friendships end?

2 Samuel 1: 1 - 12   David heard the news of Jonathan's death and he couldn't believe it, not Jonathan! He cried and wailed his song of lament in 2 Samuel 1: 17 - 27. David's love and friendship for Jonathan was stronger than the love of some men for their wives.

*For thought...*It has been said that a man's number one recreational partner is his wife. Why is it important to have both a relationship with your spouse as a "friend," someone with whom you do fun things, and to also have guy friends? Is it also important for a husband and wife to have mutual friends? Why or why not?

2 Samuel 9   True to his promise to Jonathan, David some years later asked if any descendants of Saul and Jonathan were still living. The answer was yes. The lame son of Jonathan, Mephibosheth, was still alive and had been in hiding for years because he feared being killed in revenge as a member of Saul's family. David, upon hearing this, brings Mephibosheth into the palace and cared for him and his family for years to come.

*For discussion…*Have you ever made a pledge or promise to a friend? Did you keep that promise you made to your friend?

THE DISCUSSION

1.) Think about the friendship between David and Jonathan. Think about your friendships. What are the characteristics of a good friendship, especially a Christian friendship?

2.) Jonathan and David became great friends. What were some of the circumstances that brought you and your friends together?

3.) David and Jonathan went through a lot of trials and difficult situations together. How do your friends help you through your trials and troubles in life? How do you help your friends through their trials and tough times in life?

4.) How important is it to have Christian friends? What impact do your Christian friends have on your day-to-day lives and decisions? What impact do your non-Christian friends have on your life?

5.) Who were the close friends of Jesus? What was special about their relationships?

THE ACTION

1.) Look around at church, at work, in the neighborhood to see if there is someone who could use a friend like you.

2.) Thank your friends for their friendship. Tell them why they mean so much to you.

3.) Take time to think about and appreciate the time you spend together with friends, especially when you celebrate life's events or holidays together.

THE PRAYER

    Thank you,
Heavenly Father, for the example of friendship between Jonathan and David. Help each of us to emulate the characteristics of friendship they displayed in their relationship. And help us to reach out to people who may be lonely or hurting and may need a friend. Amen.

CHAPTER 8

AMNON and TAMAR

"Consequences of Sexual Assault"

"...Why do you, the king's son look so haggard morning after morning? Won't you tell me?" Amnon said to him, "I'm in love with Tamar, my brother Absalom's sister."
2 SAMUEL 13: 4

One of the strongest and most important "movements" today is the "Me Too" movement. After years of sexual abuse, women are coming forward and sharing what they experienced at the hands of sexual predators. These predators have been a boss or coworker, someone in the community, a friend or even a family member or spouse. The patterns of abuse vary but there is physical, psychological, emotion and sexual abuse. This abuse is not just about sex but also about ego and power and intimidation and control. These predators use their authority, their status, their intimidation for their own gain at the expense of their victim. They violate without fear of any consequences or repercussions. Besides the story of Amnon and Tamar, there are other examples of sexual abuse and assault in the Bible. Joseph and Potiphar's wife, Susanna and the evil judges are two examples. In those two assaults, the victims were able to escape, but Tamar was not as lucky as them.

Their story...

2 Samuel 13: 1-38   King David had a lot of children, probably over twenty although only about half of them are mentioned by name in Scripture. Along with all those kids,

David had a lot of wives! With all those wives and children running around, the palace was undoubtedly a very busy place.

Amnon was one of David's sons; his mother was Abinoam. The Bible tells us that Amnon lusted after and fell in love with his half sister Tamar. Tamar's father was also King David, but her mother was Maacah. Tamar was described as being a very beautiful girl. While Scripture does not provide a detailed description of her, we can assume that she had, a beautiful face, long, black, shiny hair and a slender and attractive figure. Her mannerisms, the way she walked and interacted with other people, her smile and soft, gentle voice may have also been outward expressions of her beauty. We don't really know what attracted Amnon to her, but we know that something caught his eye and resulted in his desire for her.

For thought... It seems that in our culture today, women are sexually promoted especially in ads and on TV. Often the clothes that many women wear promotes sexual appeal and sexual attraction. Do you agree or disagree? Why do you believe sexual appeal is so important in our society today? Why is it promoted so prominently in ads and on TV?

Since Amnon and Tamar were both children of King David, they must have had some contact growing up together in the palace. Maybe the attraction of Tamar to Amnon grew over time or it just suddenly happened one day. Either way, Amnon was playing a dangerous and immoral game!

Today we view romantic love, lust or sex between family members, especially half brothers and sisters as incest. There are biological, emotional, and moral consequences for this type of relationship. In some ancient cultures' incest was common. Unfortunately, there were also horrific consequences that followed. Obviously, Amnon should never have let his emotions for his half-sister develop into a love and lust for her.

Tamar was a virgin, and should have been strictly off limits sexually to every man until she married. We can also assume that she must have been in her teens, probably anywhere between fifteen and nineteen.

For thought... What could Amnon have done to curb his sexual attraction to Tamar? If anyone begins to fall into the trap of sexual attraction to someone who should be off limits to him or her, what can be done to stop those feelings from escalating into harmful action?

This obsession, this stalking of Tamar, made Amnon really depressed. Here he loved a girl, wanted a girl, but he could not have her. Amnon had been pouting for days because he was so frustrated that there seemed to be no way that he and Tamar could have any physical contact between them. One day Amnon's cousin Jonadab heard about the sorry state Amnon was in and went to see him in the palace.

Jonadab saw the condition that Amnon was in. "You look terrible." Jonadab commented. "What's wrong? You're the king's son, you can have anything you want!" Amnon replied, "I'm smitten. This may seem crazy but I'm in love with my half-sister Tamar, you know Absalom's sister and I can't do anything about it." Jonadab chimes in: "I've seen her, she is definitely a ten! She sure is worth going after. Stop sulking. Cheer up! I think I can help you because I have a plan that will get you the girl you want. If this works, which I think it will because I've used it several times myself, you will have your Tamar. I guarantee it! Brighten up, this will be fun!" So Amnon decided to followed Jonadab's plan.

The next day Amnon stayed in bed pretending to be too sick to get up and attend to his palace duties. He sent a servant to his father, King David, telling him that he is too sick to come to the palace today. Concerned, King David left the palace and went to see his sick son. Amnon greeted his father in a low, muffled voice,

"Good morning Father. I'm sorry that you had to go through all this trouble to see me, your poor, sick son. You know that I must be really sick to stay away from my palace duties today." "What can I do for you son, to make you feel better?" King David replied. "I just need a little TLC dad. Come to think of it, I know something that would really help me feel better. Tamar makes a wonderful chicken noodle soup, and I'm sure if she made some for me and brought it to me, it would really make me feel better." David agreed, "You're right. Her soup is wonderful, just the right thing for you. I'll send her over to you along with her servants and some soup. You'll be better in no time." The plan started to unfold just as Jonadab had planned it.

So Tamar, directed by her father, took some of her soup and went to see Amnon. Tamar entered Amnon's room and saw the sorry state he was in. "Father told me to bring some of my special soup for you. I can see now how sick you really are" said Tamar. Amnon sat up in bed and said "Tamar, thanks for coming to see me. Your chicken noodle soup is just what I needed…plus seeing your beautiful smiling face. But could we eat alone? In case I get sick, I don't want any servants seeing me throw up everywhere." Tamar asked her servants to go outside into the hallway and left the two of them alone in Amnon's bedroom. Amnon continued, "Tamar, I can't get up out of bed. Could you sit right here beside me in bed and feed me? Right here. Sit right here. I'm too weak to move." As Tamar moves closer to Amnon, he knocks the bowl of soup out of her hands, grabs her by the arms and throws her onto his bed. With an evil, lustful look in his eyes and in his voice Amnon says, "Tamar, my sister, I love you, I must have you, I want to have sex with you, now!" Tamar, shivering with fright screams, "Amnon you're my brother! Don't force yourself on me. You can't do this kind of thing to a family member or any other girl in Israel. This is a horrible thing to do. Don't do this! What's going to happen to me after we have sex? I'll be disgraced, ruined as a future wife. And you, the king's son … what kind of example would it be? Please, if we're going to have sex together, at least let our father consent to our getting married first!" Amnon's heart was pounding, he was sweating profusely, he was shaking with excitement, he could not stop no matter what. He tore off her clothes and pressed his body onto hers as she cried" No, no, no…"

When Amnon was finished raping Tamar, a sudden flush came over him. This woman that he wanted, that he so desired … he finally had her but at what price? This was rape, not love. This wasn't the way it was supposed to be. They were both going to love each other, want each other. But this! It's all her fault. The way she looked, the way she walked, the way she talked--seducing men, seducing me. In anger, he jumped out of bed and threw her clothes at Tamar screaming "Get out of here you slut!" Tamar was crushed and broken. "You can't do this to me. You just can't discard me like a piece of trash. I have no future with any other man. I can only be with you now." Amnon shouts to his servants, "Get in here right now and throw this piece of garbage out. Make sure you lock the door behind you so she can't come back in." Tamar grabbed her clothes and hurriedly scrambled to get dressed as the servants were dragging her to the front door. Outside, crying, shaking, Tamar grabbed her veil, a symbol that she wore in public signifying she was a virgin and threw it on the ground, no longer able to wear it in public. She couldn't go back to the palace in disgrace. Where could she go? Everyone would have wondered what happened to her. She decided the only place she felt safe to go to was her brother Absalom's house.

As Absalom came to the door, he immediately sees the panic, the tears, and pain in his sister's face. Absalom cries, "Oh no. Not him. I heard you were going to see Amnon. He did this to you…didn't he? I'll kill him for this! Come in. I'll take care of you. You'll be okay. We'll get through this together. We'll keep this between brother and sister." Absalom put his gentle arms around Tamar as she continues to sob on his shoulder. Tamar listened to Absalom's advice and kept quiet about the attack. But it took a toll on Tamar. Day after day, she just sat in the corner of her bedroom quietly crying. She had no husband, no family, no future. She was alone with only her memory of that awful day.

Somehow King David heard about Amnon and his attack on Tamar. He was enraged! How could his own son do such a thing his own sister! Yet he didn't do anything about it. Amnon was supposed to be king one day ... David's firstborn. If the news of Amnon's attack on Tamar got out, what would the people think? They certainly wouldn't want Amnon to be their king. What kind of king would Amnon be after he did something like this? Then what would happen to David's family? Absalom is enraged, too, and decided to stay clear of Amnon ... at least for a while. His rage eventually turned into a plan for revenge for what Amnon did to his sister.

For thought...Families, companies, governments, universities and even the church has tried to cover up sexual assaults by leaders or members of their organizations. Why? Why have we taken so long to respond to victims of sexual assault when it has been going on for years right around us? What can we do in our families, our work place, our churches to protect and prepare women(and men!) against sexual assault?

After two years, Absalom decided that it was time for him to take his revenge against Amnon for what he did to Tamar. The perfect opportunity finally surfaced. It was festival time in Israel, the time when the blessings of God for His people were celebrated. Absalom had a particularly good year with his sheep and crops. So much so, that he decided to throw a party and invite his father, King David. King David was grateful for the invitation but declined because he would feel compelled to invite the entire palace staff, which would have been too many people for Absalom to feed. Absalom suggested to his father, "Since you can't make it, why don't you send Amnon as your palace and family representative? I would really be hurt my feelings if no one from the palace family came to my party." David replies, "Does he have to come to your party? Amnon of all people? I didn't think you liked him. I never see you two together in the palace or anywhere else. But if it makes you happy, I'll send him." Amnon heard about the party but wasn't comfortable going to see Absalom alone, so he took three of his brothers with him.

The party was going well. There was lots to eat and drink. Everyone was laughing and having a good time. After several hours of eating and drinking the time was right for Absalom to exact his revenge on Amnon for what he did to his sister. Absalom jumps up from his couch and shouts "Now!" Immediately two of his servants pounce on Amnon as he is reclining at his table and stab him repeatedly until he was dead. There was blood everywhere. People were screaming, food, cups of wine were flying around the room. Everywhere people were running to get out of there, utter chaos. Amnon's brothers were in shock. They were stunned and couldn't believe what they had just witnessed. They wondered if they would be next. Covered in Amnon's blood they jumped up and bolted for the door, heading back to Jerusalem as fast as they could get there. Fearing for their own lives, they continually looked over their shoulders to see if any assassins were after them.

News of the attack traveled fast, so fast that it reached King David before his sons made it back to the palace. It was reported that Amnon and all his brothers were murdered. The king was heartbroken, so heartbroken that he tore his clothes as a sign of grief. But when Jonadab heard the news of the attack, he rushed to the palace to have an audience with King David, his uncle. He reported to the king, "All your sons are not dead. There is only one reason that Amnon is dead. He's the one who raped your daughter, Tamar. Do you remember that? It happened two years ago. How could you forget that! I'll bet Absalom was planning this revenge all these years. He did it." Jonadab didn't mention to King David that the plan for the rape was his idea! Finally, David's other sons, brothers of Amnon, showed up at the palace. The sons were exhausted and frightened telling their father King David about what happened and their harrowing experience. They were all crying, crying not only for Amnon but that they might be killed also! David was crying not only for Amnon but also for Absalom because after the assassination, Absalom fled the country, fleeing from justice going into hiding in his uncle's nearby country. King David lost two sons that day, one murdered, one in exile. If only he would have addressed and held Amnon accountable for what he did that terrible day to Tamar, things would have been different.

THE DISCUSSION

1.) Is there a way to recognize sexual predators or situations before they might happen?

2.) Why do we make it so difficult for women to come forward to report some kind of abuse? Why are women so ashamed or afraid to report their rape or sexual assault?

3.) Why do sexual predators need to abuse, control, intimidate women? Why do they believe that they can get away with it with no consequences?

4.) How can we encourage women to come forward about their abuse experiences?

5.) What can we do to support and help victims of sexual assault heal?

THE ACTION

1.) Talk with the girls and women (and appropriately aged children) in your family about the signs and dangers of sexual predators.

2.) Support community or church programs that minister to abused women.

3.) Encourage laws and persecution of sexual predators.

THE PRAYER

Dear Heavenly Father,
We ask for Your protection for all women at home, at work, in the community from sexual predators. Help them to realize and escape from dangerous situations. Also work in the hearts and minds of those who are or would be sexual predators to cleanse them. Heal them from the wounds and feelings that perpetuate the awful urge to inflict themselves sexually onto another. And finally help victims of sexual assault heal from their wounds through Your love and the love of family and friends. In Jesus' name, Amen.

CHAPTER 9

AHAB and JEZEBEL

"The King and Queen of Evil"

There was never anyone like Ahab, who sold himself to do evil in the sight of the Lord, urged on by Jezebel his wife. He behaved in the vilest manner by going after idols like the Amorites the Lord drove out before Israel.
1 KINGS 21: 25-26

In the 1930's the entire Midwest was terrorized by a duo of bank robbers and murders…Bonnie and Clyde. Within a short period of time, they made it to the top of America's most wanted list and were finally gunned down by law enforcement officers. The hurt and pain caused by those two evil people together was unmatched in U.S. crime history. We can only imagine what havoc the Biblical duo of Ahab and Jezebel would have done in a modern era. Like Bonnie and Clyde their legacy was a trail of robbery and murder, but not as common criminals but as the king and queen of Israel!

Their story…

1 Kings 16: 29 – 34 Ahab was crowned king of Israel. Israel and Judah were at that time divided kingdoms: Judah in the south; Israel in the north. Ahab reigned as king of Israel for twenty two years and did more evil during his reign than any other king of Israel before him. He married a foreign woman named Jezebel, daughter of a pagan king. Ahab allowed Jezebel to set up temples where she worshipped her god, Baal, instead of worshipping the true God of Israel. In addition,

King Ahab ordered the rebuilding of the city of Jericho, which was contrary to God's command in Joshua 6:16. Because of this evil act, his sons Abiram and Segub died during the construction and rebuilding of Jericho, a curse from God.

For thought...Why would God let such an evil king like Ahab rule for so long? Why does God allow evil leaders to rule countries in our world today? How can you tell if a government leader is evil and acting contrary to God's laws?

1 Kings 18: 16 - 40   The prophet Elijah challenged eight hundred prophets of Baal and Asherah to a contest. The contest was made to determine which god was the most powerful, Baal or The Lord God of Israel. The prophets of Baal and Asherah went first. They prepared sacrifices, chanted, yelled and even cut themselves to try to get the attention of their gods, but nothing worked. Their god could not light their sacrifice on fire. Then it was Elijah's turn. Elijah looked up into heaven and called upon God. He prayed to God, and God heard his prayer sending down fire from heaven that consumed not only the wood of the sacrifice but also the water poured around it. Not only that, but the fire even consumed the stones and the entire earth altar! All the people who witnessed the power of God were convinced that the Lord God of Israel was the one true God. Elijah then ordered the evil prophets of Baal and Asherah to be put to death.

For thought...The people of Israel turned away from the true God and worshipped foreign gods. How important is it that our country is a Christian nation? Does it need to be? Why or why not?

1 Kings 19: 1 – 2   Jezebel is furious that Elijah killed all her pagan prophets of Baal. She made a vow to kill Elijah for what he had done. She immediately sent out an assassination squad to hunt Elijah down.

*For discussion...*It sometimes seems that the moral fiber of our society has all but disappeared. There seems to be a widening gap between what is considered morally right in our society and the moral standard that God has written in His Word. Do we as Christians ever face "persecution" by people in our society because of our Christian beliefs? How do we stand up for our Christian values when they come in conflict with societies morals?

1 Kings 21: 1 – 24   It was right next to the palace ... the most beautiful and productive vineyard in all of Israel, but it did not belong to King Ahab. Every day Ahab looked out his window and pouted that he, the king, did not own the best vineyard in his own country. He couldn't stand it any longer, he had to have that vineyard. His wife, Jezebel, noticed his frustration "Ahab, you are the mighty king of Israel. You can have anything you want. Stop pouting, cheer up. Trust me, I think I know just the way to get Naboth's vineyard for you. Sit down and eat your lunch." The next day Queen Jezebel launches her plan. First she created a false indictment against Naboth, the owner of the vineyard, and then, had him stoned as a blasphemer. Now the way was open for the vineyard to be acquired by King Ahab and Jezebel! Though they now had the coveted vineyard, it came at a terrible price...murder! Elijah, knowing what had happened, confronted Ahab and Jezebel about their evil deed. Elijah pronounced their punishment. All of Ahab's descendants will die off, and there will be an end to the future generations of Ahab's family as rulers of Israel As for Jezebel, Elijah told her that she would die and wild dogs would eat her body.

*For thought...*When our spouse is caught in a sin, or has hurt another person, how can we help are spouse change their sinful or hurtful behavior?

1 Kings 22: 29 - 38   Ahab and Jehoshaphat, the king of Judah, join together as allies in a battle against the king of Aram. Out of cowardice, Ahab disguises himself as a regular soldier so he won't be a special target singled out by the enemy. Still, Ahab is struck by a fluke arrow and killed.

*For thought...*Why do officials in government or business or even the church try to deny or cover up their mistakes, incompetence, corruption and abuse?

1 Kings 22: 51- 53   Ahab's son, Ahaziah, became king of Israel after his father's death. And like his father and mother, he also does evil in the sight of the Lord and renews the worship of Baal in Israel.

*For thought...*Why would Ahaziah follow in the evil footsteps of his parents? Was he blinded to their sin? Was he so calloused that he did not realize the hurt and damage their evil deeds did to the people of Israel and to God? Does the United States ever act contrary to His laws? How do we recognize that? What can we do about that?

2 Kings 8:16 - 19   Jehoram was now king of Judah. He even goes so far as to marry a daughter of Ahab and Jezebel. And like Ahaziah, Jehoram did evil in God's sight. By this time in the history of God's chosen people, the evil influence of Ahab and Jezebel had spread to both the Kingdom of Israel and the Kingdom of Judah.

For thought... How did God bring good out of the reign of Jehoram, even though he also did evil in the sight of the Lord? (a hint...Matt.1:8)

2 Kings 9: 30 - 37   Jehu (2 Kings 9:1 - 13) is anointed king of Israel and leads a revolt against the house of Ahab, killing everyone in Ahab's entire family. Jehu next goes in search of Jezebel the last surviving family member of Ahab and finds her at the palace in Jezreel. As Jehu pulls up in front of the palace in his chariot, he spies Jezebel looking out a second story window at him. She cries out "My what a great king killer you are. Did you come here to pay me a visit?" Jehu stops his chariot, looks up at Jezebel and shouts "You two guys, yes you two behind the curtain. As king, I order you to throw her out the window into the street. Do it now!" Two servants immediately grab Jezebel, throw her screaming through the window splattering on the stone pavement on the street below where a pack of wild dogs of the city begin to eat her dead body and licked up her splattered blood.

For thought... God is described as being a just God. Why should we trust that God will deal with evil or corrupt leaders with justice?

THE DISCUSSION

1.) As leaders of Israel, Ahab and Jezebel abused their power, acquired wealth, lived immoral lives, and committed sinful, heinous crimes. They were not very good examples of Godly rulers. What character traits do we look for in leaders of our government? Is it possible to be a good leader in our government without being a moral, upright person? Explain your answer.

2.) What is our responsibility as Christians if our government leaders (and our laws) act in ways that are contrary to our Christian faith and beliefs?

3.) Ahab married a foreign woman who worshipped Baal instead of the Lord. What are the challenges for a Christian man or woman who marries a non-Christian, someone who does not believe in Jesus or who practices another religion?

4.) Ahab and Jezebel passed on their evil legacy to their sons and daughters. How could they have broken this cycle of sin by their parents against Israel and God? How can we today break this same cycle of sin in our families?

5.) We deal with "evil" people every day at work, at school, in the community or even at church! How should we deal with people that bully others, say or do hurtful things, and have no moral character ?

THE ACTION

1.) Support politicians and laws that respect and support the values of our Christian faith.

2.) Pray for courage and conviction to stand up against people that do evil or hurtful things to us or to anyone.

3.) Look at your own life. Do you have any bad or harmful traits or habits in your life that may cause hurt or pain to other people. Ask God to show you what those habits are. Ask the Holy Spirit to change your behavior so you do not continue to hurt yourself or others.

THE PRAYER

Dear Heavenly Father,
Help us to recognize and stand up against evil and sin in the world around us. Help us to live out our Christian values in our country, our communities, and in our families. May our legacy that we leave behind be one of loving You and the people You put in our lives. And give us the strength to fight evil and injustice where we see it. In Jesus' Name, Amen

CHAPTER 10

MARY and JOSEPH

"The Value of Loving Parents"

When Joseph and Mary had done everything required by the law of the Lord, they returned to Galilee to their own town of Nazareth. And the Child grew and became strong; He was filled with wisdom, and the grace of God was on Him.
LUKE 2: 39-40

What do you think it was like being the parents of a perfect child? Or being the sibling of a perfect child? God was the One who chose for His perfect Son to be born into a God-fearing family with parents who would train Him in a vocation, teach Him along with their other children about God and their Jewish faith, and who would love Him. Parenting a perfect child was both an opportunity and challenge Mary and Joseph faced as the parents of Jesus. We know very little about the family life of Jesus growing up as a boy. He probably had a childhood similar to other children in Nazareth at that time. After Joseph and Mary were married, Joseph only appears in the story of the birth of Jesus and again in the temple incident thirteen years later. Besides being mentioned in Scripture in the recording of those events, Mary is also mentioned as being involved in the ministry of Jesus. And, she was an eyewitness to the crucifixion and resurrection of Jesus. Mary served the early church along with Jesus' brothers, James and Jude.

Their Story...

Luke 1: 26 - 38 Can't you just imagine what Mary's experience must have been like? One afternoon as she was walking back home after a hard day helping with the harvest, a figure of a man, a man dressed in dazzling white clothes, suddenly appeared right before her! Startled, she dropped her bundle of wheat from her trembling hands. This figure of a man was Gabriel, an angel of God. He spoke softly, yet with authority, "Hello Mary. You are a very special young woman; you are faithful to all of God's teachings and you love God with all your heart." Still trembling and somewhat paralyzed by fear, Mary can't quite get her mind around who this guy is and what is happening to her." Don't be afraid, Mary. I have come as a messenger from God. Mary, you will conceive and give birth to a son and you will name Him Jesus. He will be the Deliverer of Israel, the Son of God. He will sit on the throne of David, reigning over God's people. His kingdom will last forever." Mary tried to quickly sort through the jumbled thoughts in her mind to get a grasp of what the angel was saying, "Wait a minute," she replied, "Joseph and I are engaged, but we're not married yet. We have not spent a night together. I'm a virgin." The angel answered, "The Holy Spirit of God will pass into you and by His power you will conceive. The child will be the holy Son of God. And to show you the Lord's power and favor, He empowered your cousin Elizabeth, who was well past the physical age of having children, to get pregnant. She is due in about three months. What I am telling you is true and is going to happen!" Mary bowed down and responded, "I worship the Lord my God. I believe you came from Him and what you told me will happen." As Mary raised her eyes and looked up, the angel was gone! She calmly picked up her bundle of wheat and wondered, "Why me?"

For thought…Why do you think God chose Mary to be the mother of Jesus? Ladies…If Gabriel came to you as he came to Mary, what would you have thought?

Luke 1: 39 - 56 Mary could hardly wait to go see Elizabeth for herself. She traveled with a group of people to the town where Elizabeth and her husband Zechariah lived. When she arrived at their house, she knocked on the door and waited outside with a sense of expectation and excitement. As Elizabeth pulled open the door, Mary could instantly see Elizabeth's bulging belly! "Elizabeth, you really are pregnant!" Mary and Elizabeth embrace, excited to see each other and so amazed about Elizabeth's being pregnant. "Mary, come in and sit down after your long trip, we have a lot to talk about." As Mary stepped inside, Elizabeth felt a strange movement and sensation from within her womb. She sensed something was different about herself and that there was something different about Mary, too. "Mary, I can feel the Holy Spirit in me, in my baby." As those words rolled off her tongue, Elizabeth reached out to touch Mary. "You are pregnant, too! God has blessed us both but you, Mary, have received the greatest blessing. The Promised One is growing in your womb. You, Mary, have been chosen by God from among all the women ever born to be His mother, and I get to witness this. As soon as I saw you, I felt my baby move inside me as if he knew whose child you are carrying. I thank God for the promise He gave to me and to you." With those words freshly planted in her mind and heart, Mary then prays the "Magnificat," her prayer of praise and thanks to God.

For thought…We know that Mary was pregnant with the Son of God. Elizabeth was pregnant with a very special baby, too! Who was he? Later in his life, what did Jesus say about Elizabeth's baby?

Matthew 1: 1 - 17 It was foretold that the Messiah would come from the House of David. In his Gospel, Matthew traces the genealogy of Jesus all the way from Abraham to Joseph and Mary. It is an interesting list of people, identifying women, scoundrels, and saints!

*For thought...*Why such a vast array of people and personalities in the genealogy of Jesus? Wouldn't you think they would all be saints?

Matthew 1: 18 - 25 What about Joseph's story? Think about what it might have been like for him ...When Mary returned home after seeing Elizabeth, Joseph probably ran out of his shop to welcome her home, give her a big hug and kiss. But when he sees her, he is devastated. Mary is pregnant! He can't believe it! How could she do this to him? He thought she loved him. He stopped dead in his tracks; his eyes filled with tears as he looked in disbelief at Mary. Mary also with tears in her eyes trembles "Joseph wait. We need to talk." How devastated Mary must have been as Joseph turned around, ran back to his shop, and slammed the door behind him. Joseph was numb. He didn't know what to do or how to respond to Mary. That night as Joseph laid down trying to sleep, he was tossing and turning, couldn't sleep, all the while trying to get his mind around what to do. Then, suddenly, he saw a man in what appeared to be a dream. The man spoke, "Joseph, I am an angel from the Lord your God. The baby in Mary's womb was conceived by the power of the Holy Spirit of God. Marry her; you love her and she loves you. She will have a baby boy; name Him Jesus, He will save Israel and all people from their sins." Joseph jumped up, sweating profusely. "What just happened? What did I see? What did I hear? What did I just experience? A baby from God? How is this possible? This is crazy." The next day as soon as the sun came up, he went to see Mary. He took her in his arms, looked at her directly in the eye and said, "Mary, no matter how strange it sounds, how impossible it seems, I want you to hear about what happened to you at Elizabeth's and I want to tell you about what happened to me last night. You won't believe it!"

For thought…Mary and Joseph compared their experiences with each other and realized something special had happened to each of them. But what about the other people around them…Mary and Joseph's families, friends, and neighbors? What did they think about Mary's being pregnant but not yet married to Joseph? What did they think about Joseph's part in Mary being pregnant?

Luke 2: 1 - 20
The Christmas story. Mary and Joseph had a very difficult journey from Nazareth to Bethlehem. Mary was nine months pregnant and ready to deliver the baby growing inside of her at any minute. Riding up and down the hills of Judea on the back of a donkey had to have been very difficult. In addition to that, Mary and Joseph were poor and unable to pay for lodging along the way, so they slept in open fields at night and may have had only a small amount to eat. When they finally got to Bethlehem, there was no place for them to stay. Every available space was taken. They tried every where to find a place to stay. Mary was going into labor and then…the inn keeper offered them the lowly, dirty stable next to his inn. That very night … was the night that God chose for Jesus, the Savior of the World, to be born! At the very moment He was born, heavenly hosts of angels proclaimed His birth giving glory to God. Nearby shepherds in the hills around Bethlehem heard the declaration of the angels and went immediately to see this special child lying in a manger.

For thought…The shepherds played a very important role in the Christmas story. What was it? Why them?

Luke 2: 21 - 38 As good Jewish parents, Mary and Joseph brought Jesus to the temple to be circumcised and consecrated according to Jewish religious custom. At the temple, they met Simeon, a God-fearing man who had been promised by God that he would see the Messiah before he died. When Simeon saw Jesus, he knew he had seen the Promised One. In response, he gave a beautiful song of praise and thanks to God, and then he blessed both the child Jesus and His parents. But he also told Mary that Jesus would have an impact on everyone in Israel and that she, herself, would suffer much hurt and pain as the mother of Jesus. As they were leaving the temple, a prophetess named Anna also blessed the baby Jesus and prophesied to Mary and Joseph that this child would be the redemption of Israel.

For thought... As Mary watched her beloved Son, Jesus, being crucified and hanging on the cross, what words of Simeon do you think she may have remembered? Could she have ever imagined that this would be the hurt and pain she would suffer as the mother of Jesus?

Matthew 2: 13 - 18 When King Herod heard about a baby born in Bethlehem that was destined to be the king of Israel, he was determined to keep that from happening. He was so jealous that he dispatched a squadron of soldiers to Bethlehem to kill every baby boy born there. His plan was to eliminate any possibility that there could be a child who might survive to be king one day. But before the soldiers arrived, Joseph was warned in a dream to get out of Bethlehem and hide in Egypt where Herod's men could not find them.

For thought... People were trying to kill Jesus almost His whole life. (They finally did succeed!) How do you think those assassination attempts on His life effected Him?

Matthew 2:19 - 23 (Luke 2: 51 - 52) About three years later, after King Herod died, Joseph, Mary and Jesus returned to live and work in Nazareth, their home town. Jesus grew in wisdom and stature. He was loved by His parents and by the people of Nazareth, and by God.

*For thought…*Mary and Joseph returned back home to Nazareth, their home town, after having been gone for several years. They may have even returned with more children than just Jesus. After being gone for so long, what kind of reception do you believe the people of Nazareth would have given them? Were the people of Nazareth glad to see the "Holy Family" come home?

Luke 2: 41 - 50 When Jesus was twelve years old, Mary and Joseph took Him to Jerusalem to celebrate the Feast of the Passover. After the feast was over, the caravan left Jerusalem and started back to Nazareth. At the end of the first day of travel, Mary and Joseph began to round up their family for dinner. It was assumed by them that Jesus was in the caravan with relatives. But when they begin to search for Him, they can't find Him. (Home Alone?) After frantically searching the caravan, they went all the way back to Jerusalem looking for Him. For three days and three nights they searched continually for Jesus. Finally, they found Him. Perhaps they caught a glimpse of Him or perhaps they heard His voice as He stood in the temple among a group of priests and teachers. As Joseph and Mary frantically push their way through the crowd, there He is! They must have said a quick prayer of thanksgiving that He was safe and sound. Undoubtedly, they ran up to Him and hugged Him first. But, then, Mary asked, "Jesus, where have You been all this time. Your father and I have been worried sick about You. Why didn't You come home with us as we asked you to?" Jesus replied" You don't have to worry about

Me, mom. I'm here in the temple where I belong. I love it here! I'm OK." As any mother who had been so frightened and worried might do, Mary responded sternly: "Belong in the temple...not! You belong back home in Nazareth with your family. It's time now to go home. Now, let's go! This time stick with your father until we get home."

THE DISCUSSION

1.) Why did Jesus need a set of earthly parents? What might Jesus have experienced growing up with His parents Mary and Joseph and His brothers and sisters?

2.) From the other family members point of view…What would it be like being the parents of the perfect child, Jesus? What was the experience of Jesus' brothers and sisters growing up with an older brother like Jesus? How would you feel being the sibling of Jesus growing up together?

3.) Mary and Joseph certainly were loving parents for Jesus and all His brothers and sisters. What are the responsibilities of Christian parents for their children?

4.) How can we as parents and grandparents pass on our Christian values to our children and grandchildren?

5.) What are some of the major challenges that our children face in today's world? What can we do to equip our children to live out their Christian values and meet the challenges of today?

THE ACTION

1.) Think about your childhood growing up. What did your parents do (or maybe not do!) to bring you up in the Christian faith.

2.) Talk with your spouse; develop a plan for raising your children in the Christian faith (if you have not already done that).

3.) When your children are the appropriate age, talk with them about the importance of meeting and marrying a Christian spouse.

THE PRAYER

Dear Heavenly Father,
Thank You or providing God-fearing parents for Jesus during His life on earth. Thank you, Lord, for our parents and family who love us and brought us to Jesus. We ask that You guide us as parents to love our children and bring them up in the knowledge of Jesus as Lord and Savior. Amen.

CHAPTER 11

SIMEON and ANNA

"Patience and Prayer"

> Now there was a man in Jerusalem called Simeon, who was righteous and devout…he would not die before he had seen the Lord's Messiah.
> LUKE 2: 25-26

> There was also a prophetess Anna…she gave thanks to God and spoke about the Child…
> LUKE 2: 36-38

God please help me… now! That's how we usually pray. We need immediate help, immediate answers right now! We are an "instant needs" society and want results now! We can't wait in line; we can't wait in traffic; we can't wait for test results; and we rush to the "no waiting aisle five." Some of our prayers do result in God's immediate attention and answer for help or healing or guidance. But often we are told by God to wait. He doesn't always answer our prayers immediately according to our time frame. We need to be patient and wait to hear God's answer to our prayer. Part of our praying process is patience. We need to continue to pray and trust God while patiently waiting for His answer. Sometimes having patience and trust is the answer to our prayer! Talk about patient prayer … Anna prayed in the temple for over fifty years! We don't know how long Simeon prayed, but we assumed it was for a long time also. God answers every prayer…but when? That is up to Him!

Their story...

Luke 2: 22-40 After Jesus was born, Mary and Joseph observed the Jewish religious custom of having their baby boy circumcised and then presenting him and announcing his name at the town synagogue. So after Jesus was born and named, they traveled to the temple in Jerusalem after Mary's purification time to present Jesus to the Lord in observance of the Jewish law. They were to offer as a sacrifice two doves or pigeons, according to Leviticus 12:8. As the priest was releasing the sacrifice for Joseph and Mary's firstborn, an old, disheveled looking man who was sitting along the colonnade in the temple area heard the priest say the name "Jesus." This man named Simeon immediately jumped up and his heart started pounding. A rush of excitement suddenly came over him. This is it ... this is the day! Finally, after all these years, all these years, He is finally here! Simeon was a good man, a religious man, a man who devoted his life to prayer and worshipping God. One night many, many years earlier the Holy Spirit came to Simeon and said, "Simeon, you are a man who has devoted his life to praising God. Because you worship God with a pure heart and spirit, you will see the Promised One, The Deliver, The Messiah before you die."

Simeon saw Mary and Joseph and the baby Jesus as they were walking through the temple court after His consecration. Simeon knew that this was the baby, this was the Messiah to be. Simeon walked up to Mary and Joseph and asked, "May I see your child? He's beautiful. May I hold him? I have a blessing for Him." At first Mary and Joseph wondered who this old man was. But they could sense an excitement and a sincerity in his voice, so Mary gently handed baby Jesus to Simeon. Simeon was so excited that he could hardly contain himself. Shaking, with voice quivering, he prayed a prayer of thanksgiving: "Dear Lord, You promised me that one day I would see the Messiah before I die, and I know that today is that day. Every day I prayed that this day would be the day, and now it's here; I can die in peace with Your fulfilled promise in my heart. I see right here before me that this child will bring both glory to You and salvation for the people of Israel. He will bring salvation for all people of every nation, both Jews and Gentiles."

*For thought…*In some worship settings we recite the words of Simeon. What special meaning do these words have for us today?

Mary and Joseph were stunned by his words. As Simeon handed the baby back to Mary, he looked into Mary's eyes and put his hand on the heart of Jesus. "This child will cause both many to come to God and many to reject Him. The true heart for God of many people will be revealed by Him. His life will one day cause you great hurt and pain to you His mother." Mary and Joseph turned and slowly walked away in awe of his words and blessing (and warning!). Simeon extended his arms and looked up to heaven and shouted, "Blessed are You oh Lord God, Creator of the universe. Great is Your mercy and greatly You are praised!"

But just as Mary and Joseph and the baby were walking away about to leave the temple, an old woman, haggard in her face, wearing clothes that were faded and worn, came up to them and put her hand on baby Jesus. Looking up to heaven, she prayed: "Thank You, almighty God, that this child will one day reconcile Israel to You." She was a widow who had been fasting and praying in the temple every day for fifty years, praying that the Messiah would come one day to deliver His people back to God.

*For thought…*How did Jesus live out the prophetic words of Anna and reconcile Israel to God?

It sure wasn't a typical day of consecration for baby Jesus or for Mary and Joseph. An old man and an old lady who were God fearing people shared some strange blessings for their baby. Joseph and Mary left the temple wondering...What does all this mean?

THE DISCUSSION

1.) Simeon and Anna were promised by God that they would see the Messiah before they died. They waited patiently; it was a long time before the promise was fulfilled. How do you remain patient while waiting for God's answer to your prayers?

2.) When God answers prayer, He sometimes says yes; He sometimes says no. Why does God sometimes say yes, and sometimes says no to our prayers?

3.) How long should you pray for God's help and guidance? Should you pray once or twice and let it go or should you pray until you get an answer to your prayer?

4.) Simeon was a righteous man; Anna was a prophetess. How does our faith and our relationship with God affect our prayer life?

5.) Share how you felt when God said "yes" to one of your prayers. Share how you felt when God said "no" to one of your prayers.

THE ACTION

1.) Look at some of the prayers in the Bible and the special way they were offered. What can you learn from those prayers. How can you apply their intent to your own prayer life.

2.) Pray to God every day thanking Him for the many blessings you receive from Him.

3.) In conversation with family or friends, or perhaps even strangers, ask if there is anything that you can pray about for them.

THE PRAYER

Dear Heavenly Father,
Thank You for the example of Simeon and Anna, who were faithful to pray and wait patiently for Your answer. Teach us to pray with patience. Help us to understand and accept Your answers ... the times when you say yes and the times when you say no. And most important of all, strengthen our faith that we grow to trust that whatever answer you give us is the right answer to our prayer. Teach us to trust that Your answer will accomplish Your purpose for our lives and will align with Your will. In Jesus' Name, Amen.

CHAPTER 12

JAMES and JOHN

"Disciples of Jesus"

> Going on from there, He saw two other brothers, James, son of Zebedee and his brother John. They were in a boat with their father Zebedee, preparing their nets. Jesus called them, and immediately they left the boat and their father and followed Him.
> MATHEW 4: 21-22

When you accepted Jesus Christ into your life as Lord and Savior, you became one of His disciples. A disciple is described as a follower of Jesus, absorbing and living out the teachings and lifestyle of Jesus. We often refer to the Twelve Apostles as the Twelve Disciples, but Jesus had many more disciples than those twelve. Though the number fluctuated, there were thousands of disciples during the time that Jesus lived on earth. Today around the world there are almost three billion disciples … all followers of Jesus!

James and his brother John were the second set of brothers called directly by Jesus to His circle of twelve, along with brothers Peter and Andrew. Their lives were instantly changed the day Jesus called them to follow Him. They experienced an incredible three years with Jesus as eye witnesses of His ministry, His death and His resurrection. James and John continued their ministry after the ascension of Jesus and both were instrumental in the growth and development of the early Christian church.

Their story...

Matthew 4: 18 - 22   Among the first disciples that Jesus called were James and John, who were fishing partners with another set of brothers, Peter and Andrew. They all lived and worked in Capernaum on the shore of the Sea of Galilee. James and John are also identified as the sons of Zebedee, a prominent businessman in their hometown.

One day early in His ministry, Jesus approached James and John while they were fishing. He called to them: "Come, follow Me, and I will make you fishers of men." They immediately dropped their fishing nets and left their family, their home, and their occupation to be followers of Jesus. It seems that the direct words of Jesus had a dramatic impact on them. In addition, they may have had some prior knowledge of who Jesus was. The reason they responded without hesitation is not completely mapped out in Scripture. But we do know they responded immediately, without hesitation, to Jesus' call and became His disciples.

For thought...How were you called to be a disciple of Jesus? Was it through your parents who brought you to church? Was it a friend, or even a stranger, who had an impact on you? Or was there a specific event that you experienced that influenced you to become a disciple of Jesus?

Mark 3: 17   James and John are referred to as "Boanerges", meaning "sons of thunder." Possibly that "name" describes their character or that it is a description of their behavior (possibly loud and boisterous behavior). Certainly, as fishermen, they were probably pretty tough guys working down on the waterfront. Perhaps they were calloused men, physically strong; yet, they needed to be molded spiritually.

For thought…Like James and John being called "Boanerges", how would you could describe your character or personality in a few words, what would they be?

Mark 9: 2 – 10 Jesus is both true man and true God. Until the time described in these verses known as the Transfiguration, James and John had however only seen Jesus as true man. When Jesus took the two of them, along with Peter, up onto a high mountain, He also revealed His identity as true God. He instantly became transfigured before their eyes and His clothes became dazzling white brighter than the sun! They were so frightened; their minds could not comprehend the experience of what was happening, Jesus revealing Himself as true God. Besides that, Moses and Elijah appeared as well! Only after Jesus died and rose from the dead, did James and John then realize the significance of this event.

For thought…What is the vital importance that Jesus is both God and man?

Luke 9: 51 – 56 When James and John (along with Jesus and the other disciples) were turned away from a village in Samaria, they were so furious at the insult that they wanted Jesus to punish that village by bringing fire down from heaven to destroy their town! (2 Kings 1: 9-10) This was certainly not their finest hour or an appropriate response to rejection. (Could this type of lightning quick, "violent" and noisy response to rejection be a reason why Jesus called James and John "Sons of Thunder"?) In defense of James and John, however, it should be noted that Jews and Samaritans had a long history of feelings of antagonism toward one another. Jesus rebuked (strong word!) James and John for their strong emotional desire to retaliate for the rebuff and rejection of Jesus and His disciples by the Samaritan villagers.

*For thought...*Why do we feel awkward or embarrassed or intimidated to share with people that we know, or people we meet, that we are a Christian and what it means to be a Christian?

Matthew 20: 20 -23   Was Mom Zebedee ambitious for her sons or did she just do what any mom would do when she put in a good word for her boys, James and John, with their teacher, Jesus. She, obviously, recognized that Jesus was destined for great things and she wanted her sons to share in His accomplishments when He came to power in Jerusalem. (To her credit, Mom Zebedee was with Mary at the foot of the cross during the crucifixion of Jesus on Good Friday.) She asked Jesus if her boys could sit at His right and at His left when He established His kingdom. If Jesus granted her request, she knew her sons would be seated in very high places of honor and authority. Jesus responded, telling her that only God the Father would decide who sat at His right and left when He came into power in His (heavenly) kingdom. Jesus went on to explain what it would mean to sit at the right or left of Him. If it were James and John, it meant they would have to live, to suffer, and to die for Jesus. Not only that, but their reward would not be in an earthly kingdom but would be in a heavenly kingdom. While Jesus spoke to James and John telling them that they did not know what they were asking for, both of them said they could drink "the cup of suffering" and were prepared to experience whatever Jesus had to experience, including suffering and death. Jesus gave them a great answer to close out their conversation. He said, "Come to think of it, yes, you will drink the cup of suffering and death like Me." And in the years ahead, James and John did suffer and die for their faith in Jesus Christ as their Lord and Savior.

For thought…Even though we are Christians, we are not immune to suffering and hardships. What do we learn as a result of hardship or difficulty in life? How does our faith as a disciple of Jesus grow through the tough times of life?

Matthew 21: 1 – 11

Jesus had just performed one of His greatest miracles, raising Lazarus from the dead. Jesus had already raised two other people from the dead earlier in His ministry. Each miracle of raising someone from death back to life was a purpose-driven demonstration of His power as the Messiah. Now at the "top of His game," Jesus and His disciples enter into Jerusalem with crowds of people cheering them on as if they had just won the Super Bowl! James and John may have thought something like, "Wow, this is it. This is why we left our homes, our families, our jobs. Jesus will be crowned king soon, and we'll get a great job in his cabinet!"

For thought…What was Jesus and the disciples thinking on Palm Sunday as all of Jerusalem was shouting His praise "Hosanna to the Son of David", when just a few days later those same people of Jerusalem on Good Friday were crying out "crucify Him!"?

Luke 22: 7 – 34

It was now Thursday evening and the celebration of Passover had begun. Jesus, along with His disciples, had spent the days prior to their celebration preaching and teaching along the streets of Jerusalem and in the temple courts. During the Last Supper shared with His disciples that evening, Jesus spoke His final words of instruction to the Twelve. Jesus told them how to serve and love others as He had served and loved them. The Gospel of John, (chapters –14-17), is a record of some of the most beautiful words of comfort and blessing Jesus shared with His disciples (and with us!) at the conclusion of the Last Supper.

The words He spoke then are sometimes referred to as His "Farewell Discourse." At that same time of blessing, Jesus also instituted the sacrament of Holy Communion, our visible remembrance of the sacrifice and forgiveness that He offers for all Christians. James and John certainly were strengthened in their faith by the words and actions of Jesus that night. Little did they know that in the coming days, weeks, and years ahead, they would need every ounce of that strength of faith in Jesus.

*For thought...*What does the blessing in John 17: 20 - 26 by Jesus to all future believers mean to you?

Mark 14: 32 – 50   Peter, James and John had a unique closeness with Jesus and were part of Jesus' "inner circle" of disciples. They were chosen to be present at special events in the ministry of Jesus while the other nine disciples were not chosen to be there. On that Thursday night when the Disciples finished their Passover dinner, Jesus and the disciples (less Judas) went to the Garden of Gethsemane. Jesus wanted to pray for strength and guidance from the Father to face the hours ahead of His suffering and death. James, John, and Peter were to pray and support Jesus in His final hours before His crucifixion. But instead, they fell asleep! Some help and support they were! It must have been very disappointing for Jesus to find His closest friends asleep when He was so deeply troubled and had specifically asked them to keep watch and pray with Him. It must have been even more disheartening to Jesus to know that one of His own beloved disciples would betray Him. When He was arrested, not one disciple stood with Jesus. Peter, impulsive Peter, reacted immediately by using a sword and cutting off the ear of one of the servants of the High Priest, but Jesus healed the servant's ear and rebuked Peter for resorting to violence. Then, James and John along with all the other disciples fled, terrified by the thought that they, too, could be arrested. Where was your courage, where was your loyalty to your teacher, your "king," your Messiah, James and

John?

*For thought...*When was there a time that you "let Jesus down" by committing a hurtful sin or when you missed an opportunity to witness for Him?

John 19: 25 - 27   Only one disciple was present at the crucifixion of Jesus, and that disciple was John. John was referred to as the "disciple whom Jesus loved," so we know that he certainly held a special place in the heart of Jesus. Here at the foot of the cross, John did show his courage, his loyalty, his devotion to Jesus as he accepted the responsibility to care for Mary, Jesus' mother.

*For thought...*Who should have been at the foot of the cross of Jesus to take care of Mary instead of John?

John 20: 1 – 10   Early on Sunday morning following the crucifixion, Mary Magdalene went to the tomb where Jesus was laid after His death and discovered that the stone was rolled away from the entrance. Frightened, she ran to tell Peter and John about what she had seen. The two of them immediately sprinted for the tomb to see for themselves. John (being younger and possibly more physically fit) got there first. The tomb was just as Mary said it was ... empty! John's heart started pounding and he was shaking with excitement. His mind was swirling with so many thoughts and memories of the past three years with Jesus. Over and over John kept thinking in his mind these words from Jesus "The Son of Man will be delivered over to the chief priests ... flogged and crucified ... on the third day He will be raised to life." John began to wonder: "Can it really be true? I see it, can I believe it!"

*For thought...*As a disciple of Jesus if you were present

that Easter morning at the tomb of Jesus like John was, what would you have thought, what would you have felt?

John 20: 19 – 23   That same Sunday night all the disciples (except for Thomas who was absent and Judas) were gathered together behind closed doors because they were afraid of being arrested like Jesus. Then suddenly Jesus appeared in person and stood among them. They were stunned. "It's really Him. It's Jesus! It is true! He really did rise from the dead!" After days of living their lives in fear, they were renewed in faith and courage by seeing, talking with and hugging Jesus, their Lord and Savior. They were ecstatic! Jesus breathed onto them the power and gift of the Holy Spirit, and they were born again ... new men! Jesus appeared another time to James and John as they were fishing one day later. They were also both present at the ascension of Jesus. Along with the other disciples, James and John received their "marching" orders for their ministry on earth. His commission to them (and to us) is found in Matthew 28:18-20: "Therefore go and make disciples of all nations, baptizing them in the name of the Father, and of the Son, and of the Holy Spirit."

*For thought...*What would it have meant to you as one of His disciples to have seen, and talked with, and touched Jesus after His resurrection?

Acts 2: 1 – 41   The Day of Pentecost described in these verses is called the "birthday" of the Christian church. The apostles were all gathered together in one place, and there was an outpouring of the Holy Spirit on them. Tongues of fire danced on their heads. Through the power of the Holy Spirit, the Disciples immediately began preaching and teaching in many languages to the Jews present that day, from all over the world, worshipping in the temple in Jerusalem. Those who were there could experience the miracle of the Disciples preaching and teaching them in their own native language! Because of the outpouring of the Holy Spirit that day, the Christian church exploded with over 3,000 believers in Jesus being baptized. Wow! These new believers in Jesus came to Jerusalem from over sixteen countries, each returning to their home filled with the Good News. We're not sure what languages James and John spoke but we do know they had a powerful life-changing testimony of their faith in Jesus Christ. We do know that all who heard and accepted the truth of the Gospel that Pentecost Day received the same life-changing faith in Jesus as their Lord and Savior.

*For thought…*How do you recognize opportunities you have every day to witness your faith or show that you are a Christian?

Acts 3:1 - 10   One day Peter and John were going to the temple to pray when they encountered a lame man begging for money at the temple gates. Filled with compassion, Peter and John looked straight at the lame man, "We don't have any money. Look at us; we're poor guys. But we do have a gift for you. It is better than any money we could give you. In the name of Jesus Christ of Nazareth, walk!" The man felt life and strength in his legs, and he got up and walked! A miracle! Yes, a miracle more precious than anything money could buy. Just having the simple, everyday gift of being able to walk. Praise God! Thank you, Peter, thank you, John, thank You, Jesus!

*For thought…*What blessings do you take for granted that you enjoy every day?

Acts 4: 1 – 22   The chief priests were upset by the miraculous healing of the lame beggar by Peter and John in the name and power of Jesus (recorded in Acts 3). They were also upset by the effect the miracle had on the people nearby who had witnessed the healing. Consequently, they arrested Peter and John and drug them before the high priest. In response to their interrogation before the chief priests, Peter and John gave a bold and powerful testimony of their faith in Jesus. It was so powerful, in fact, that the chief priests saw the courage of Peter and John and realized that they were unschooled ordinary men. They were astonished, and they took note "that these men had been with Jesus".

*For thought...*How can you be prepared to personally share your own faith story of who Jesus is and why you are a Christian in one or two sentences?.

Galatians 2: 6 – 10 Paul makes reference to John as one of the pillars of leadership in the early church. (The James mentioned here is not the brother of John but the brother of Jesus!)

*For thought...*How did James, the brother of Jesus, become a disciple? How did he then develop into a leader in the early church?

Acts 12: 1 – 2 This was a time of intense persecution of the church. James, the brother of John, was killed with the sword by the order of King Herod. James was the first and only disciple specifically mentioned as a martyr in the New Testament. (Church tradition says all the other disciples except John, were martyred for their faith. Since there was intense persecution of the leaders of the early church, it is likely that they, along with other future church leaders, were all killed.)

*For thought...*How is the Christian church being

persecuted today?

Revelation 1: 1 - 3, 9 John went on to write his Gospel account of the life of Jesus and then concluded his life by writing three epistle letters, First John, Second John, Third John. Later, he wrote the book of Revelation while exiled on the island of Patmos.

*For thought…*Revelation is a difficult book to understand. But what main lesson do we learn from the book of Revelation?

THE DISCUSSION

1.) Was there any significance of Jesus calling two sets of brothers as His disciples, James and John, along with Peter and Andrew?

2.) James and John were fishermen called to be disciples of Jesus. What is your calling, your responsibility as a disciple of Jesus?

3.) Mom Zebedee wanted a "reward" for her boys for giving up everything and following Jesus. What reward do you want for being a disciple, a follower of Jesus?

4.) If you were one of the twelve disciples, why would Jesus have chosen you and what would have been your most exciting experience as one of the twelve disciples of Jesus?

5.) Why are you a disciple of Jesus? Why did you accept His calling, "To come follow Me..."?

THE ACTION

1.) James and John gave up their family, their home, their profession. Think about what you give up on a daily basis to follow Jesus.

2.) Can your family, your friends, your coworkers tell that you are a disciple of Jesus.

3.) Tell your family members who are also disciples of Jesus how much it means to you that as a family you both share your faith in Jesus as Lord and Savior.

THE PRAYER

Dear Heavenly Father,
Thank you for the discipleship of brothers James and John. They gave up everything to follow You. Help us to "give up everything" to be Your disciple. Thank you for the gift of the Holy Spirit who called us to be disciples of Your Son Jesus. And thank You for our fellow family members who together share our faith in Jesus. In Jesus' name, Amen.

DYNAMIC DUOS of The Bible

CHAPTER 13

MARY and MARTHA

"Sisters Serving Jesus"

As Jesus and His disciples were on their way, He came to a village where a woman named Martha opened her home to them. She had a sister called Mary...
LUKE 10: 38-39A

If you have a set of sisters in your family, you know that they can be so different and yet so alike. Sisters grow up with the same set of parents, experience most of their early lives together, and share daily activities together. They grow up learning to share the same love of family, the same core values, and certainly love for each other. Although, each has her own personality, her own life perspectives, and her own unique experiences. As we look at Mary and Martha, we see two sisters with entirely different personalities and priorities. Still, they shared the same love for Jesus as their Lord and Savior.

Their story...

Luke 10: 38 – 42 How would you like to cook dinner for thirteen hungry, tired, and probably dirty men and also provide a place for them to spend the night in your home? It would be a lot of work. That was the challenge when Martha opened her home to Jesus and His disciples as they were traveling through Bethany. It is interesting to note that Luke refers to the home of Lazarus, Martha, and Mary as Martha's in His Gospel. Usually it would have been referred to as the home of Lazarus, her brother, but for some reason it seems Martha assumed the responsibilities of running the household. It has been suggested that she was the oldest of the three siblings and that may be the reason that she had responsibility for their home. It has also thought that since Martha and her siblings had a home large enough to accommodate Jesus and His disciples, they must have been fairly wealthy. In any case, Martha and Mary were familiar with Jesus because He had been teaching and preaching for some time in their area. They often hosted Jesus and served Him as a guest in their home. When they saw Jesus coming to their hometown, they were very excited and honored to invite the somewhat famous and unorthodox teacher, Jesus, to stay with them.

As Jesus and His disciples settled into Martha's home during one of their visits, they washed up and sat down to relax. Martha began to make dinner for everyone. There were no microwave ovens or modern kitchen tools like we have today, so fixing dinner was a tedious job done by hand. (As grandma called it ... from scratch!) As Martha began the dinner preparations, she wondered why Mary was not helping her. "She should be here with me in the kitchen helping to cook dinner. I can't do this all by myself; I can't make dinner for sixteen people. It will take hours." Can't you just picture it in your mind ... Martha stewing about and then storming out of the kitchen to look for her sister! When she found her, Mary was sitting right next to Jesus talking with Him and listening to His teaching. Martha was furious. She threw down her apron and walked straight up to Jesus and Mary. "Teacher," Martha said, "we practice good Jewish hospitality in our home. I'm trying to get dinner ready for everyone, but Mary isn't helping me at all! Don't You think Mary should be helping me? She shouldn't be spending her time listening to You when she has more important duties to attend to! She can listen to You later after dinner when the dishes are cleaned up. Please tell her to help me right now!" Jesus replied, "Martha, calm down. Yes, there is a lot of work to do but right now is a great opportunity to hear My teachings. Dinner can wait a minute. My teachings and time with you are very important. You won't get too many more opportunities to talk with Me in person in the future. Mary realized the importance of this opportunity with Me. She made a good choice; don't be angry with her for that. In fact, why don't you sit down next to Mary and join us? Dinner can wait. I think taking the time to learn from Me right now will have an important impact on you both."

*For thought...*What effect did this dinner with Jesus have on the attitude of Mary and Martha about how to serve and how to learn?

John 11: 1 - 44 Fast forward to the Gospel of John and another visit by Jesus to the home of Martha, Lazarus and Mary. On this visit, Jesus raised Lazarus from the dead. The raising of Lazarus from the dead is one of Jesus' greatest and most important miracles. We already know from our previous reading and study that Lazarus, Martha and Mary were very close friends of Jesus, friends that He loved. We also believe that Jesus and His disciples visited them often and stayed in their home when they were in the Bethany area. Their house in Bethany was close to Jerusalem, located in what we would consider a suburb. At a time when Jesus was across the Jordan River, preaching and teaching some distance from Bethany, Mary and Martha tried to reach Him with the news that Lazarus was very ill and near death. When Jesus finally heard the news, He told His disciples, "This sickness will not be the end of Lazarus; he won't die. God will be glorified as a result of what will happen." Jesus and His disciples stayed two more days where they were across the Jordan River before beginning the journey to Bethany, in the region of Judea. Some of the disciples were a little nervous and anxious about crossing back into Judea. "Teacher" they said, "Some of the Pharisees were trying to kill You there. It will be very dangerous for You, and for us, to go back there." Jesus assured them that He knew what He was doing, so they began to journey toward Bethany.

After they had walked some distance, Jesus, knowing that Lazarus had already died, encouraged them: "Our friend Lazarus is sleeping and I'm going to wake him up." Jesus meant that Lazarus was sleeping in death, not taking a nap. The disciples did not understand and thought that Jesus would just wake him from his sleep to heal him. Jesus stops in His tracks, turns around directly at them and emphatically tells them, "Lazarus is dead. For your benefit, I stayed here two extra days. What you witness will be life changing for you all." Then Thomas bravely (Bravely? Thomas?) confessed: "We've faced danger before and if it means getting killed with You, Teacher, we're with You 100% no matter what happens."

For thought...Why were the Pharisees out to kill Jesus during his entire three year ministry? What threat was Jesus to them?

When Jesus and His disciples arrived in Bethany, there was a lot of commotion. There were all kinds of people crying and mourning outside Martha and Mary's house because Lazarus had died four days earlier. When Martha learned that Jesus had arrived, she rushed out to see Him and talk to Him: "Lord, if You had come while Lazarus was still sick, You could have healed him like You healed so many other people. But even though Lazarus is dead, I believe God is with You and He will honor anything You ask of Him." Wow! Martha, way to go! What an example of trust and belief in Jesus. What a beautiful testimonial of faith. Jesus looked Martha straight in the eye, and put His arms on her shoulders. "Your brother will rise again." "Yes," responded Martha. "I believe in the resurrection of all of us." Jesus continued, "I am the resurrection and the life. The one who believes in Me will live, even though they die; and whoever lives by believing in Me will never die. Martha, do you believe this?" With tears streaming down her cheeks, she confessed, "Yes, Lord, I believe that You are the Messiah, the Son of God, who has to come into the world".

For thought... Only one other person gave a testimony like Martha's. Who was it?

Martha turned around and went back to the house to get Mary, "Mary, Jesus wants to see you." Mary immediately jumped up and ran out of the house to see Jesus. When she reached Him, she collapsed on the ground, sobbing at His feet. "Lord, if You had been here while Lazarus was sick, you could have cured him. He would not be dead now." Jesus slowly lifted Mary up with His loving arms around her and whispered, "Where is he buried?" She glanced over her shoulder past the crowd to a hill about a hundred yards away. A friend of Mary's offered to take Jesus to the place where Lazarus was buried. As they were walking to the tomb, Jesus could not hold back His own tears any longer. He could feel the hurt and the pain of sin and death in the lives of His friends, a family He loved. Everyone, even those who knew who Jesus was thought that it was too late to heal Lazarus; he was dead. Jesus had healed the sick and blind. He had performed amazing miracles. Still, everyone wondered what could be done for Lazarus since he was already dead.

Jesus steadied Himself in front of the tomb that had been carved into the side of a hill with a stone covering the entrance. Jesus told the men there: "Take the stone away from the entrance to the tomb." Martha protested. "Lord, Lazarus has been dead four days and his body is decaying already. There will be a bad smell." Jesus said to her: "Didn't I tell you that if You believe in Me and what I can do, God will be glorified here today." As they rolled away the stone covering the entrance to the tomb, Jesus opened His arms and looked up to heaven. "Father, thank You for hearing My prayer to You. You always answer My prayers according to Your will. The people here are witnessing My prayer to You and this miracle. It will have a profound effect on their faith in Me." Jesus stepped forward and shouted" Lazarus, come out!" Slowly, the crowd began to see a figure wrapped in linen cloth coming out of the tomb. It was Lazarus! Stunned, their minds could not comprehend that a man who had been dead for four days was walking out of the tomb! (People in those days knew about death. In fact, they saw it up close and personal almost every day.) With their hearts pounding and tears of joy flowing, Martha and Mary rushed to Lazarus and removed the strips of burial cloth from him. All three of them embraced, hugging and kissing each other. Even they were struggling to understand and believe what they had just experienced. They turned around and saw Jesus standing there with tears in His eyes. He had performed another miracle ... for them! He raised Lazarus from the dead. Jesus of Nazareth was, indeed, the Messiah and their Lord and Savior.

*For Thought...*How were the lives of Lazarus, of Mary, of Martha changed after this miraculous event?

John 12: 1 - 8 Jesus and His disciples shared another meal together in the home of Lazarus, Mary and Martha. It is recorded in the Gospel of John and occurred shortly before the triumphal entry of Jesus into Jerusalem on Palm Sunday. Just as she had been before when Jesus came, Martha was in the kitchen getting dinner ready. Lazarus was talking with Jesus in another room when Mary entered. She stooped down at the feet of Jesus and poured expensive, wonderful, fragrant perfume over His feet. (Feet were very special in those days. People walked everywhere, mainly in sandals, and places where it was not very sanitary.) As she poured the perfume on the feet of Jesus, she loosened her long hair and used it to wipe His feet dry. What a sign of reverence, what a sign of worship Mary showed for her Savior. Incensed at her extravagance, Judas objected with strong words: "Wait a minute. We could have sold that perfume for a lot of money and used it to help the poor." (Of course, we know Judas' motive was not to help the poor, but to help himself to the money.) Jesus responded and addressed everyone there. "Leave her alone. There will always be poor people who will need our help. Mary has done a beautiful thing for me. She was saving this perfume for my burial ceremony one day. But instead of waiting until I die to pour it on Me, she has used it now while I am alive to honor Me."

For thought...This was right before Jesus' entry into Jerusalem on Palm Sunday. Do you believe that Mary may have had a premonition about the coming death of Jesus?

THE DISCUSSION

1.) Martha and Mary had different priorities in serving Jesus. Martha made dinner; Mary listened to His teachings. Why is it important to be both a Mary and a Martha ... to learn more about Jesus like Mary and to serve Jesus like Martha?

2.) What effect did the words of Jesus in Luke 10:41-42 have on Mary? On Martha?

3.) How do you demonstrate that you have made serving a priority, as Martha did? How do you demonstrate you have made learning a priority, like Mary did?

4.) When Mary anointed Jesus with perfume, she honored Jesus as her Lord and Savior. How do your lifestyle and actions honor Jesus as your Lord and Savior?

5.) How do you remain humble in your service to Jesus and His church when you do a good job? How do you respond to someone who compliments you when you serve the church?

THE ACTION

1.) Like Mary, look for ways this week, to learn more about Jesus as Lord and Savior.

2.) Like Martha, look for ways this week, to better serve Jesus and His church.

3.) Write a testimonial of faith. Explain why Jesus is the highest priority in your life.

THE PRAYER

Dear Heavenly Father,
Give us hearts that desire a closer relationship with You. Instill in us a desire to learn more about Your gift of salvation for us. Mold our hearts; guide us to use our time, our talents, our treasure, and our opportunities each day to serve You and Your church. Make us examples of Your love to others. Amen.

CHAPTER 14

ANANIAS and SAPPHIRA

"A Life of Hypocrisy"

> Then Peter said, "Ananias, how is it that Satan has so filled your heart that you have lied to the Holy Spirit and have kept for yourself some of the money you received for the land?"
> ACTS 5: 3

One area of criticism of the Christian church today by non-Christians is based on what is believed to be the hypocritical lifestyle of some Christians. Non-Christians think that Christians want to look so pious and holy going to church every Sunday yet, as soon as they leave church, their actions during the week are anything but Christ-like. Yes, we are all sinners, even Christians. However, how Christians live out their day-to-day lives matters. Non-Christians, especially, pay close attention on how we live each day. Jesus tells us that we are supposed be "in the world" but not "of the world." In other words, Christians are supposed to be different. Christians represent Christ Himself and as such should be examples of honest, loving and giving people. When Christians don't act in a way that is perceived by non-Christians to be Christ-like, the label "hypocrite" is sometimes associated with us. Most Christians go to church on Sunday to worship because they recognize that they are sinners and are in need of God's grace and forgiveness. They don't go to look pious and holy. However, there have always been some Christians who go to church for their own benefit wanting to look pious and holy but are not. Ananias and Sapphira were those people. They were a classic example of Christians who were hypocrites.

They wanted to be included as part of the church looking holy and pious, but they were not Christ-like in their relationship with Jesus. They suffered the consequences of their actions.

Their story...

Acts 5:1-11   As the early church was growing, the members devoted themselves to teaching, to fellowship, to prayer, to sharing everything together. They sold property and possessions to give to anyone who had need. (Acts 2) Joseph, a Levite from Cyprus, called Barnabas, sold a field he owned and brought the money and put it at the apostles' feet. (Acts 4) Christians were coming together every day to pray together, to worship together, to make sure their fellow believers had food and clothing and a place to stay, the necessities of life. Some Christians, like Barnabas, even sold their family land so that the money could be used to help those in need.

*For thought...*Read Acts 2:42-47. How does your local congregation emulate the example of the early church in this passage?

One Sunday believers in Jesus were gathering together for worship and fellowship in a member's home. It was a special day because the Apostle Peter was going to join their group and share his experiences and teachings. Quite a large crowd was gathered there that morning. Ananias, one of the believers, knew that Peter would be at the meeting, and he suspected that there would be a large crowd there, too. As people were gathering together for worship, Ananias waited until the last minute to "strut up" in front of the gathering. In his heart he was hoping that he would be seen by all those who were there. Just as everyone was sitting down, Ananias got up to announce: "Peter, it is an honor for you to be here with us. We are a small, humble group of believers and we are grateful that you would take time out of your busy schedule and grace us with your presence today. In honor of your coming to visit us today, my wife Sapphira and I sold our family vacation home for $250,000. Here is the money from the sale. Please take this "small" gift from us and use it to help our poor fellow believers in need." Ananias placed the bag of money in front of Peter. Then he leaned slightly forward to bow and lowered his head. Although his body language suggested a humble posture, he displayed a pompous grin on his face. Ananias sat down beaming with pride from his most generous action. The members of their small group gasped at the amount of the gift, $250,000! No one had ever donated that much money to the church. Wow! They were in awe that Ananias and Sapphira were such an extreme example of Christian love in action because this was the most generous gift ever made for the needy.

Peter then got up slowly and picked up the bag of money Ananias had given him. He walked straight over to where Ananias was sitting. Ananias assumed that Peter was going to give him a special blessing and gratefully acknowledge their generous gift to the church in front of everybody there. "Surely," Ananias thought to himself, "Peter will use this act of Sapphira and I as an example to all the congregations that he visits. Surely, he will tell them of our extreme generosity." Ananias looked directly up at Peter. Peter wasn't smiling. Instead, he had sadness and disappointment written all over his face, which then turned to anger. Peter tosses the bag of money at Ananias. Gold coins spilled everywhere. Everyone there was shocked by Peter's reaction, most of all Ananias! With firmness and conviction in his voice, Peter exclaimed "Ananias, you are lying! You didn't sell your home for $250,000. You sold it for $350,000. You made it sound as if you gave the entire amount to the church. You held back $100,000 for yourselves. You are a hypocrite! You did an evil thing; you lied to us here and you lied to God. We thought you were so filled with the Holy Spirit that it moved you to give this gift, but it didn't. Sin guided you to do this for your own glory, not God's glory! Now, I am sorry but you will have to suffer the consequences for your actions." At that instant Ananias grabbed his throat, gasped his last breath and fell backwards dead! Everyone there jumped up. Their hearts were racing. Everyone was trembling and wondering what had just happened!

For thought...What is the difference between sacrificial giving and giving out of our excess?

Peter goes back to his seat and sits down. Some of the stronger young men picked up Ananias' body and carried it outside where he was then buried. Everyone there finally settled down and realized the seriousness of Ananias' action. He lied to both men and to God.

You can't do that without consequences. We are to be honest before men and have an honest heart for God. We are to look for honor from God and not from men.

For thought...In Malachi 3:10, God promises to bless us if we "bring the whole tithe into the storehouse." What does that mean? What blessings do we receive for doing this?

Later in the day Sapphira came to the house to attend the meeting. Like her husband Ananias, she was anticipating all the accolades she thought she would receive for her generous gift to the church. But, instead, as she walked into the room all faces were glued onto her and they were not happy. Peter stood up and asked, "Sapphira, did you sell your vacation home for $250,000 like Ananias said you did?" Sapphira looked around but didn't see Ananias anywhere in the room. She had expected a warm greeting with everyone patting her on the back. She now knew something was wrong. Still, she chose to lie. She replied,

"Why yes, Peter, the selling price of the vacation home was $250,000. Wasn't that among the most generous donation you have ever received for the church?" Instead of commending her, Peter spoke words that he received from the Holy Spirit "You and your husband lied and sinned against the Holy Spirit. You gave only a portion of the selling price of your vacation home and your motivation was to elevate yourselves. You wanted the glory for yourselves and not for God. You get the same punishment as your husband." With those words, Sapphira too fell over dead. Within a few hours, both Ananias and Sapphira were gone. Instead of earning the reward and glory they sought for themselves, God gave them a different "reward," justice for their hypocrisy. They became an example for the early church and for us that God, and God alone, deserves the glory and honor of our actions. We all learned that the Holy Spirit cannot be fooled. God knows what is in your heart.

For thought…Why is it important to give not only your treasure in service to God and His church, but also to give your time and talents as well?

THE DISCUSSION

1.) What is your motivation for giving your time, your talent and your treasure to God's church?

2.) When someone at church gives you a compliment on a job well done, how do you feel? Is it okay to feel good about serving God and His church?

3.) How do you keep a humble attitude when you serve the church?

4.) Are we as Christians sometimes guilty of being hypocrites? Do our actions during the week match our piety on Sunday? What happens when they don't match?

5.) What do you say to non-Christians who may call us Christians a bunch of hypocrites?

THE ACTION

1.) Read Luke 18 about the Pharisee and the Tax Collector.

2.) Put into action the words of Jesus when He says, "First take the log out of your own eye and then you will see clearly to take the speck out of your brother's eye."

3.) Think about how you can use the blessings and resources that God gave you to better serve His church.

THE PRAYER

Dear Heavenly Father,
Forgive us when we look for glory for ourselves when the glory should go to You. Help us to serve You humbly and to give generously of our time, our talent and our treasure to serve You and to help others in need. In Jesus' Name, Amen.

CHAPTER 15

AQUILA and PRISCILLA

"Partners in Life, Partners in Ministry"

"Greet Priscilla and Aquila, my co-workers in Christ Jesus. They risked their lives for me. Not only I but all the churches of the Gentiles are grateful to them."
ROMANS 16: 3-4

There are lots of married couples mentioned in Scripture but none of them had a greater influence on the growth of the early church than Aquila and Priscilla. Not only were they partners in marriage but they were also missionary partners helping to establish churches in Corinth and Ephesus. By their example of faith as a couple, they not only impacted the churches they served, but they also helped to develop the future leaders of the Christian church in the world.

Their story...

Acts 18: 1 – 3 During Paul's second missionary journey he had a vision of a man from Macedonia (recorded in Acts 16:9). The man was standing and begging Paul: "Come over to Macedonia and help us!" Realizing that this vision was from God, Paul immediately changed his mission focus to Macedonia, which was the northern part of Greece, located between the Adriatic and Aegean Seas. Paul, along with Silas and Timothy, began their new journey at Philippi and continued south to cities that included Berea, Thessalonica, and Athens. One of their last stops was the city of Corinth.

For thought... What was one significant accomplishment about Paul's going to Macedonia? What was the impact on his ministry by going there? What was the impact on the early church?

Corinth was an important trading center of the Mediterranean area and a cosmopolitan center of close to 100,000 people. Corinth also had a significant Jewish population so there were many Jewish synagogues there. But one of the most prominent buildings of worship in Corinth was the Temple of Aphrodite, dedicated to the goddess of love. As part of the pagan worship at that temple, over 1,000 prostitutes engaged in sex orgies with people who came to worship there.

As was his custom when he stayed in a city, Paul went to the market place in the center of town. He set up shop as a tent maker, being thankful that God had given him a skill that allowed him to support himself when he was traveling and preaching. Besides that, setting up shop in the center of the city market place gave Paul an excellent opportunity to meet people in a comfortable and business-like setting, witnessing to them about Jesus.

It was in the city of Corinth that Paul met Aquila and Priscilla. Scripture does not say how Paul met them, but it does say that both Paul and Aquila and Priscilla were tent makers and that he stayed and worked with them. Because of persecution and an eviction order by the Roman Emperor Claudius, Aquila and Priscilla had been forced to leave Rome a few years earlier, settling in Corinth. Aquila and Priscilla may have come to faith after meeting Paul or they may have already had some previous knowledge of Jesus. There were up to 40,000 Jews living in Rome at that time so it is probable that some word about Jesus must have reached Rome before

Aquila and Priscilla left. (It is recorded in Acts 2 that there were Jews from Rome attending the Pentecost festival in Jerusalem who heard Peter's message. They were among the 3,000 baptized that day!)

For thought…Who are some other couples mentioned in the Bible? What were some of the strengths and what were some of the challenges they faced in their marriage and lives?

Acts 18: 18 – 19   Paul stayed about a year and a-half in Corinth before leaving to go to Ephesus along with Aquila and Priscilla. What they experienced during those eighteen months with Paul must have changed the lives of Aquila and Priscilla so dramatically that they left their home in Corinth and accompanied Paul to a new city and a new calling as missionaries. It is likely that Aquila and Pricilla were somewhat acquainted with Ephesus because they were from an area of Pontus, about 300 miles east of Ephesus.

It is also likely that Aquila and Priscilla were of some financial means since they were able to move, travel, and establish homes in four different cities. There is no mention of children so we can assume that either they did not have children or their children were grown and on their own when they met the Apostle Paul. While Paul and Aquila were busy making and repairing tents, it was a great opportunity for Priscilla, to daily witness about Jesus to the women who came to the market to shop. Luke mentions Priscilla's name before her husband's name several times in the Book of Acts. It could have been his intent to either give both she and Aquila equal credit for their missionary work or perhaps Priscilla played a larger role in their missionary outreach than her husband did. In either case, Priscilla, by her witness and example, made it clear that God's gift of salvation through Christ Jesus was available to all people … man, woman or child. Each would be welcomed into the family of God and a new life to those who declared their faith in Jesus.

Paul saw great potential in this loving couple and taught them the truths of God and what it means to be a believer. What a blessing it must have been for Aquila and Priscilla to live and work so closely with Paul and observe him "in action" for those eighteen months in Corinth. During that time Aquila and Priscilla obviously developed an enthusiastic zeal to follow his example and to spread the message of the Gospel to others. With confidence, Paul sent them out to lead a new church in Ephesus and entrusted them with the responsibility to instruct and develop new leaders of the church there.

Acts 18: 24 – 28   While in Ephesus, Aquila and Priscilla met Apollos, a Jewish man who was a Christian. Scripture doesn't tell us for sure, but he may have been a disciple of John the Baptist. Scripture does tell us that Apollos knew of the baptism of John, and he had knowledge of Jesus. We also know that he fervently believed that Jesus of Nazareth was the Messiah. After meeting Apollos in the local synagogue, Aquila and Priscilla were impressed with his eloquent speech and fervor for the Gospel of Jesus Christ. They realized, however, that he was lacking in some critical doctrinal knowledge, possibly knowledge about the baptism of the Holy Spirit. They capitalized on the opportunity to personally share with him "the way of God more accurately."

Romans 16: 3 - 4   In his letter to the Roman Christians, Paul paid tribute to the courage of Priscilla and Aquila who risked their lives alongside Paul as missionaries and early leaders of the church. Both Corinth and Ephesus were dangerous places to preach the Good News, (1 Corinthians 15:30-32) especially Paul's passionate preaching to Gentiles in those communities.

Perhaps because of the rampant prostitution and infidelity in Corinth, Paul felt compelled to share God's plan for marriage in his letters to believers in both Corinth and Ephesus. While it is generally believed that Paul was never married, there are some Bible scholars who suggest that he may have been married at some point in his life. Paul was a Jewish Pharisee and was "zealous" about strictly adhering to Jewish law and tradition. Marriage was viewed as an important religious responsibility by the Pharisees. In either case, we know that he was not married at the time he wrote his letter to the Christians in Corinth (1 Corinthians 7:8-9). Whether he was married or not, Paul must have been grateful that God had provided Christian friends and co-workers, Aquila and Priscilla, who were committed to moral excellence in their marriage. The marriage of Aquila and Priscilla was characterized by kindness, charity, forgiveness, devotion and love. They were faithful to keep the commitments they had made to one another before God, especially in matters of sexual intimacy within the marriage only. It was evident that Aquila and Priscilla felt the love that Jesus had for them and His Church and they wanted to live out that same kind of love within their marriage.

For thought... Paul worked with some remarkable women in his ministry...Lydia, Priscilla, Eunice, Lois, and others. What guidelines does Paul give to us about women serving in the church? How can we support more women serving in God's church?

1 Corinthians 16: 19 - 20

Paul again mentioned Aquila and Pricilla, sending their greetings to the Corinthian Christians from the church in Asia that met in their home. The early Christians had no synagogues or buildings to gather for worship, so they started worshiping in their own homes. Groups of several ... or even up to twenty or thirty Christians, would come together to worship and fellowship with one another. In Acts 2, Luke recorded that when they gathered, they would sing a hymn or Psalm, share a meal together, and pray. The Lord added to their number daily, and their home church grew. They were a Christian family, sharing the same faith in Jesus and devoting their lives to serving each other. They shared their material possessions with each other and shared the Good News of salvation in Jesus with everyone they met. What better place than your home to make new friends, new Christians feel welcomed and comfortable.

Aquila and Priscilla were very hospitable. They had a caring, friendly, sincere way of inviting people into their home and introducing them to Jesus. They accepted everyone and served everyone, wanting nothing in return. They took Peter's words of instruction to heart: "Offer hospitality to others ... God has given you so much, pass those blessings on to everyone."

Peter's words are important for us, too. We should all be hospitable, gladly, cheerfully, opening up our homes to others, not as an obligation but as an opportunity to witness to others. Perhaps we should each carry the gift of hospitality even further and take that caring, that act of hospitality and kindness on the road. Why not consider visiting the shut-in, the elderly, the disabled, those in jail or in hospitals. Helping people who are just lonely and hurting, needing to experience your love and the love of Jesus.

For thought... There is an emphasis in many congregations on small groups. What are the benefits of having small groups in your congregation, and what are the benefits of your being in a small group?

2 Timothy 4:19   Writing to Timothy in Ephesus (1 Timothy 1:3), Paul extends his greetings to his dear friends in Christ, Aquila and Priscilla. They are now in Ephesus with Timothy. Like Apollos, young Timothy must have spent countless hours of study and discussion with Aquila and Priscilla concerning their faith and how to reach all people, Jew or Gentile with the saving grace of Jesus Christ.

THE DISCUSSION

1.) Are there unique benefits of serving God's church as a married couple? What are they? How can you support the faith, the ministry of other married couples in your congregation?

2.) Why is it important for Christian married couples to support the faith of their spouse? What are some of the challenges that Christian couples face today?

3.) If you are married, or single, what are some ways that you can practice the gift of hospitality? Who do you know, friend, neighbor or co-worker, that you could invite to your home?

4.) What makes having a Christian spouse so special? If your spouse is not a Christian, what affect does that have on your faith? On your marriage?

5.) When God calls a husband or wife to a mission or a ministry in the church, why is it a calling actually for the both of you?

THE ACTION

1.) God says to give our time and care to our family the first priority. Discuss with your spouse setting "boundaries" concerning the time and effort you commit to serving the church

2.) Think about what missions or ministry, you serve in at church. Discuss with your spouse why you feel the calling to serve in that mission or ministry. If you are married, how can you support your spouse in the area of ministry or mission where he/she serves.

3.) If you are married, discuss ways you can work together as a couple to reach family, friends, co-workers, and neighbors for Jesus.

THE PRAYER

Heavenly Father,
Thank You for the example of Priscilla and Aquila as a loving, caring couple serving each other and serving your church. May we open our hearts, open our homes to welcome people into our lives as Aquila and Priscilla did. Fill us with a genuine concern for others; help us to build relationships with those outside our immediate circle of friends. Give us boldness to share Your gift of love and salvation with them so they might become members of Your heavenly family. In Jesus' Name, Amen.

DYNAMIC DUOS of The Bible

CHAPTER 16

PAUL and TIMOTHY

"Training Church Leaders"

"Timothy, my son, I am giving you this command in keeping with the prophecies once made about you, so that by recalling them you may fight the battle well, holding onto the faith and a good conscience."
1 TIMOTHY 1: 18-19A

As the early church grew in numbers, it became apparent that some form of organization and future leadership was needed to guide its members. The first generation of church leaders, mainly the twelve disciples and others like Paul, were both getting older and were suffering from years of intense persecution. It was time to solidify the doctrines and teachings of the new Christian faith and identify future church leaders. Paul, James, John and other disciples began to write down the principles of faith so they could accurately be shared with future generations of believers. At that time, Paul was greatly impressed with a young man who had a strong foundation of faith. His name was Timothy. Paul took Timothy as his apprentice and gave us an example of how to train church leaders that we still use today.

Their story…

Acts 16: 1 - 5 On Paul's second missionary journey he came to the city of Lystra. There he met a young man named Timothy who was known to have a strong faith, passed on to him through the teaching of his mother and grandmother. Paul invited Timothy to join him on his next missionary journey, along with Silas. During that missionary journey, Timothy stayed with Paul and helped him preach and teach in Philippi, Thessalonica, Athens, Corinth and Ephesus.

1 Corinthians 4: 14 – 17 Paul sent Timothy as his personal representative to the church in Corinth. The Corinthian Christians had moved away from correct teaching and doctrine taught to them by Paul on an earlier journey to Corinth. Paul sent Timothy with a glowing recommendation, loving him like a son who is faithful to the Lord and well versed in the teachings of Scripture and the Christian faith. He later asked the church leaders in Corinth (1 Corinthians 16: 10 - 11) to watch over Timothy, especially because of his young age, so that no physical harm would come to him.

*For thought…*What specific things can your congregation, your denomination, do to give support and guidance to new, young pastors and church workers?

Philippians 1, Colossians 1, Philemon 1 These are three of Paul's prison letters, written while he was under house arrest in Rome. In the opening verses of these chapters of Scripture, Paul addressed his greetings to the churches and individuals along with a greeting from Timothy. Timothy must have come to Rome on several occasions to be with Paul while he was in prison.

*For thought…*What was one possible "downside" of being Paul's apprentice? What trials, what hardships did Timothy have to endure along with Paul?

Philippians 2: 19 – 24 Paul instructed the Philippians to receive Timothy graciously because he had a genuine caring and affection for them. Paul vouches for the work of Timothy, describing it as a son learning a trade from his father. He told the Philippians that Timothy would love and care for them with the same genuine affection that Paul had for them. Paul also told them of his hope to visit the church in Philippi after his imprisonment in Rome comes to an end.

1 Thessalonians 3:1-6 Timothy was sent to Thessalonica to encourage the church there and strengthen them in the faith and knowledge of the teachings of the Gospel. After doing as Paul had asked, Timothy then returned to him in Athens with good news about how the love and faith of those in Thessalonica was growing each day. Timothy also shared the desire of his Thessalonian friends for Paul to personally come and visit them.

1 Timothy 1:1-2 and 2 Timothy 1:1-2 Both of these letters written by Paul are specifically addressed to Timothy as the pastor of the church in Ephesus. Throughout these two letters, Paul encourages and instructs Timothy on how to teach, to preach, and to lead the church, especially in the face of growing challenges of persecution and false doctrine.

*For thought...*One of Paul's greatest concerns was that correct doctrine be taught to all Christians. What was Timothy's responsibility in the protection of church doctrine?

1 Timothy 1: 3–7, 18 Paul told Timothy of the importance that he stay in Ephesus to stand up against men who were wandering away from the true faith and teaching false doctrine. He encouraged Timothy to have a sincere faith, a loving heart, and a clear conscience. Paul reminded Timothy about his "charge" and responsibilities as a pastor, received from the Holy Spirit and prophesied about him.

1 Timothy 3:14-15 Paul clearly stated that the intention of this letter was not only to instruct Timothy in his role as a leader of the church, but it was intended to instruct all future church leaders regarding their appropriate roles in the church and with regard to their Christian behavior.

1 Timothy 4:12-16 Timothy had a strong faith as a young man. He needed to remain confident in his faith and carry out his duties in a manner that served to glorify God and be an example to other leaders and believers. It was especially important for Timothy to use his spiritual gifts received from the Holy Spirit at the laying on of hands by the church elders. Paul knew that Timothy's belief and actions would have a definite influence on the faith and salvation of others.

*For thought...*Being a pastor's spouse or being the spouse of a church worker can be difficult and demanding. How can your denomination, your congregation, support the wellness of church workers' families?

2 Timothy 1:13-14, 2 Timothy 2:1-2, 2 Timothy 3:10-17 In all these verses, Paul affirms the extreme importance of Timothy's role as a future church leader. He reiterates that Timothy has learned the correct teachings directly from him. Timothy has become well-qualified as a pastor and leader in the church, as he has emulated Paul's lifestyle and teachings.

THE DISCUSSION

1.) Why did Paul choose Timothy as his protégé, what did he see in Timothy's faith and character? Why did Timothy accept the assignment and the responsibility of being Paul's protégé?

2.) Timothy was greatly influenced by the faith of his mother and grandmother. We can assume that they probably encouraged Timothy to go with Paul. Is there anyone in your family you can encourage and support as he/she considers going into the ministry or into any other leadership position in the church?

3.) What is the responsibility of the Christian church, your denomination and your local congregation in training new pastors and church leaders?

4.) How did Timothy show his love and respect for Paul? How do we show our love and respect for our congregational pastors and church workers?

5.) What qualifications and characteristics do you look for in your pastor and church leaders?

THE ACTION

1.) Write a note of thanks and encouragement to your pastor.

2.) Support your denomination's seminaries.

3.) Be a role model and mentor to a younger or newer church member.

THE PRAYER

Dear Heavenly Father,
Thank You for the relationship of Paul and Timothy and their example of mentoring and training church leaders. Help us to daily pray for and support our pastors and encourage faith-filled men and women to choose ministry to Your church as their careers. When our congregation is looking for a new pastor or church leaders, give us the wisdom to choose the right people of faith and character to meet the needs of our church. In Jesus' name Amen

FINAL THOUGHTS

Whoever God partners you with in life, be it a spouse, a friend, a coworker, fellow church member, be your own "Dynamic Duo". Live your partnership by doing your best for each other, complimenting and helping each other, accomplishing together small and large contributions to God's church and His people.

God put the people in this study together for His purpose, whether to achieve good or show evil. There are so many life and faith lessons from this study. We need to learn from the positive and negative actions of these duos and apply them directly into our lives. That's the value of this study, how the lives of ordinary people in the Bible effect our actions today.

Hopefully this book showed you how the "Dynamic Duos" served God's church, learned to forgive, to be humble, to be an instrument of God, to fight sin and evil, to grow God's church. May God bless your study of "Dynamic Duos of the Bible" and help you grow in your relationship with Jesus Christ as Lord and Savior.

DYNAMIC DUOS of The Bible

SOURCES

1. Achtemeier, Paul J., Harpers Bible Dictionary. Harper and Row.1985
2. Arterburn, Stephen, Merrill, Dean. Every Man's Bible. Tyndale House Publishers, Inc. 2014
3. Bowker, John. The Complete Bible Handbook. DK Publishing. Inc. 1998.
4. Bricker, Charles, et al. Jesus and His Times. Readers Digest Association, Inc. 1987.
5. Crawford, Vaughn E., et al. Great People of the Bible and How They Lived.3rd. Readers Digest Association, Inc. 1974.
6. Dowley, Tim. The Crossway Illustrated Bible Handbook. LionHudson plc.2005
7. Flory, Marjorie, et al. Illustrated Dictionary of Bible Life and Times. Readers Digest Association. 1997
8. Freedman, David N. et al Who's Who in the Bible. Readers Digest Association, Inc. 1994
9. George, Jim. The Bare Bones Bible Bio. Harvest House Publishers. 2008.
10. George, Jim. The Bare Bones Bible Facts. Harvest House Publishers. 2009
11. George, Jim. The Bare Bones Bible Handbook. Harvest House Publishers. 2006
12. Graf, David, et al. ABC's of the Bible: Intriguing Questions and Answers About the Greatest Book Ever Written. Readers Digest Association, Inc. 1991
13. Peterson, Eugene H. The Message: The Bible in Contemporary Language. Navpress. 2003

DYNAMIC DUOS of The Bible

ABOUT THE AUTHOR

Glenn Sprich and his wife Patti live in St. Louis, Missouri. Both are retired and stay very busy with their four children and nine grandchildren. Patti has served as a parish health nurse and she currently leads a grief share support group. Glenn is active in leading a small group and Sunday morning Bible class. They are members of the Lutheran Church of Webster Gardens in Webster Groves, Missouri.

www.ingramcontent.com/pod-product-compliance
Lightning Source LLC
Chambersburg PA
CBHW070851050426
42453CB00012B/2140